PIANO PRONTO®

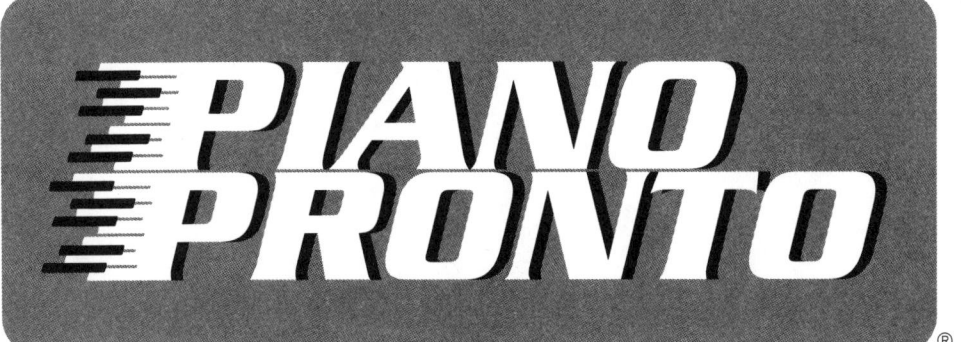

Movement 3

(Level 3)

Written and Arranged by

Jennifer Eklund

PIANO PRONTO PUBLISHING

www.PianoPronto.com

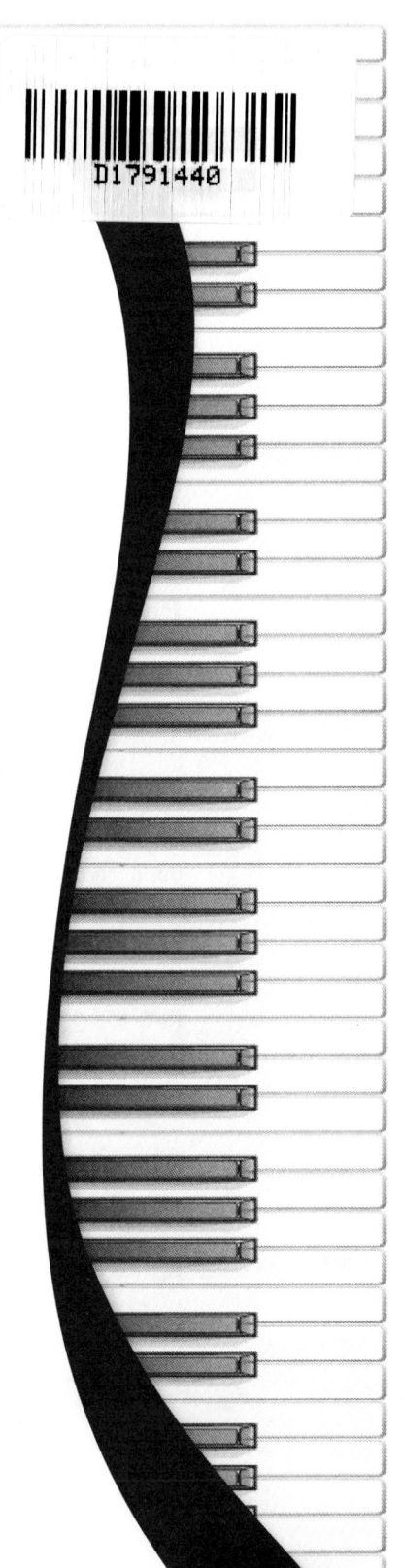

Piano Pronto:Movement 3

Jennifer Eklund

Copyright ©2008 by Jennifer Eklund. All Rights Reserved.

WARNING: The compositions, arrangements, text, and graphics in this publication are protected by copyright law. No part of this work may be duplicated or reprinted without the prior consent of the author.

ISBN 978-0-9818616-3-0

Printed in the United States of America

Piano Pronto Publishing
PianoPronto.com

Design: Chaz DeSimone
DesimoneDesign.com

Movement 3
TABLE OF CONTENTS

BLUE DANUBE *(Strauss)* 2
MOZART MEDLEY *(Mozart)* 6
BOURREE *(Bach)* 12
LULLABY *(Brahms)* 15
THURSDAY BLUES *(Eklund)* 17
SAKURA *(Japanese Traditional)* 21
SAINT ANTHONY CHORALE *(Haydn)* 24
IN THE HALL OF THE MOUNTAIN KING *(Grieg)* 28
CHOPIN MEDLEY *(Chopin)* 32
THE ENTERTAINER *(Joplin)* 36
MEDLEY OF VOCAL CLASSICS *(Mozart / Giordani)* 39
SPRING THEME NO. 3 *(Vivaldi)* 43
LIEBESTRAUM *(Liszt)* 47
B-FLAT MAJOR SCALE 50
ITALIAN AIR *(Traditional)* 51
BLUES MEDLEY *(Traditional)* 53
THE ARKANSAS TRAVELER *(Traditional)* 58
HUNGARIAN RHAPSODY NO. 2 *(Liszt)* 62
G MINOR SCALE 64
SWAN LAKE *(Tchaikovsky)* 66
DANCE OF THE HOURS *(Ponchielli)* 70
MEDLEY OF ITALIAN SONGS *(Capua / Cottrau)* 73
CAPRICE *(Paganini)* 78
SYMPHONY NO. 40 THEME *(Mozart)* 81
JE TE VEUX *(Satie)* 86
FÜR ELISE *(Beethoven)* 90

PIANO PRONTO

WELCOME TO MOVEMENT 3

PRONTO PREP

Play the examples below to help prepare for "*Blue Danube Waltz.*"

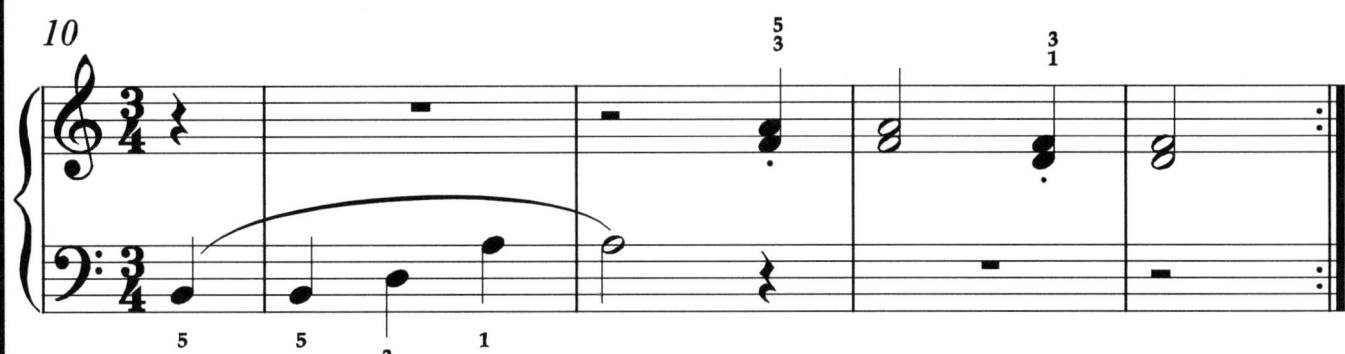

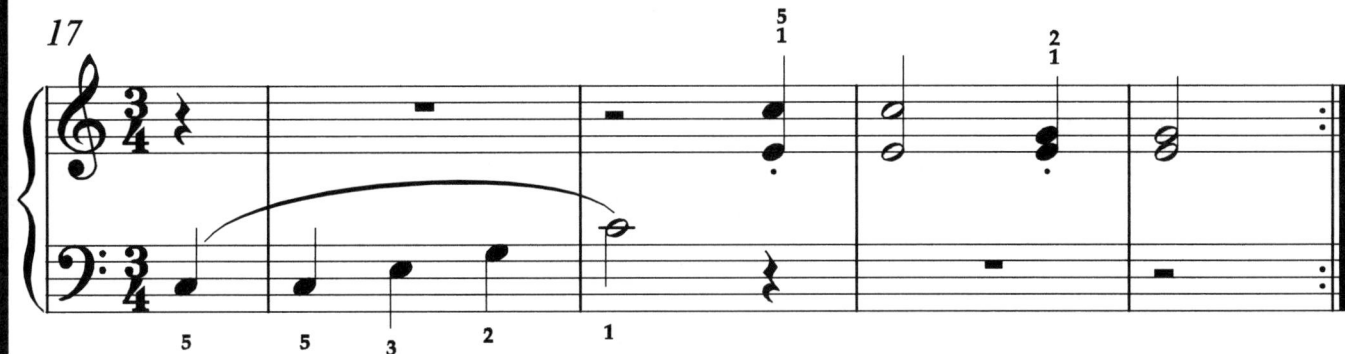

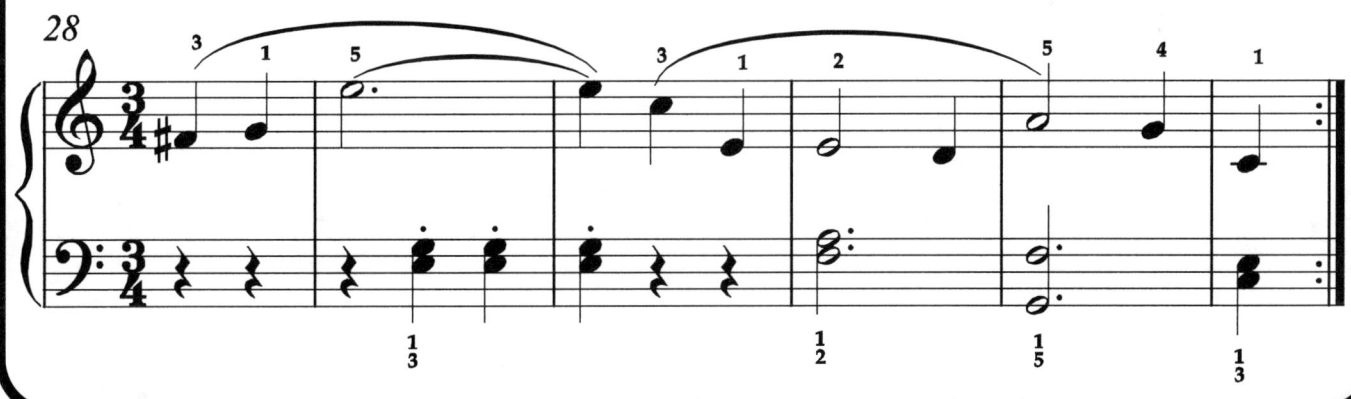

BEFORE YOU BEGIN:

- *Which hand plays the **melody**?* Right   Left   Both

- *The next piece is in the **key of**:* _____

Blue Danube Waltz

Johann Strauss, Jr.
Arr. Jennifer Eklund

Moderato

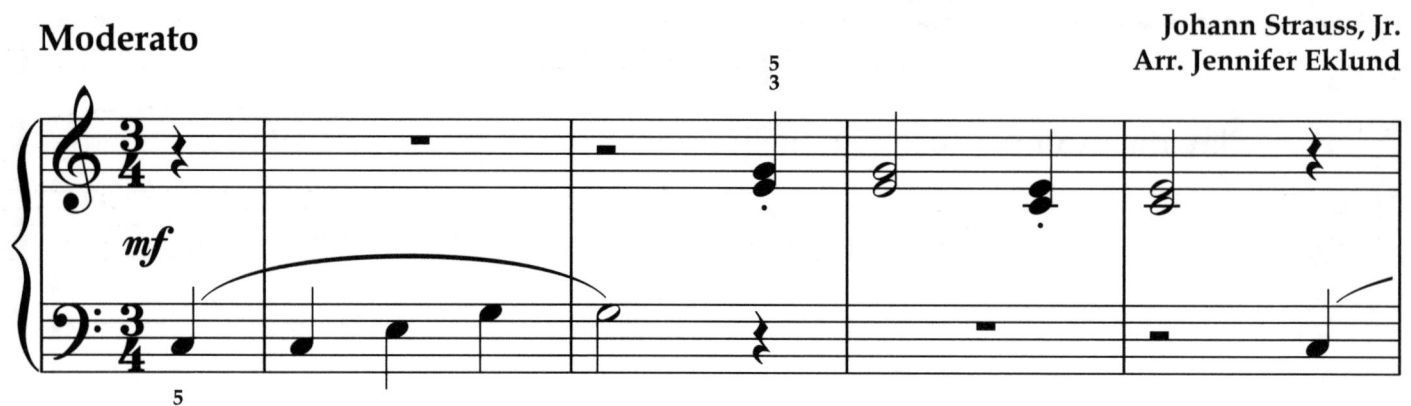
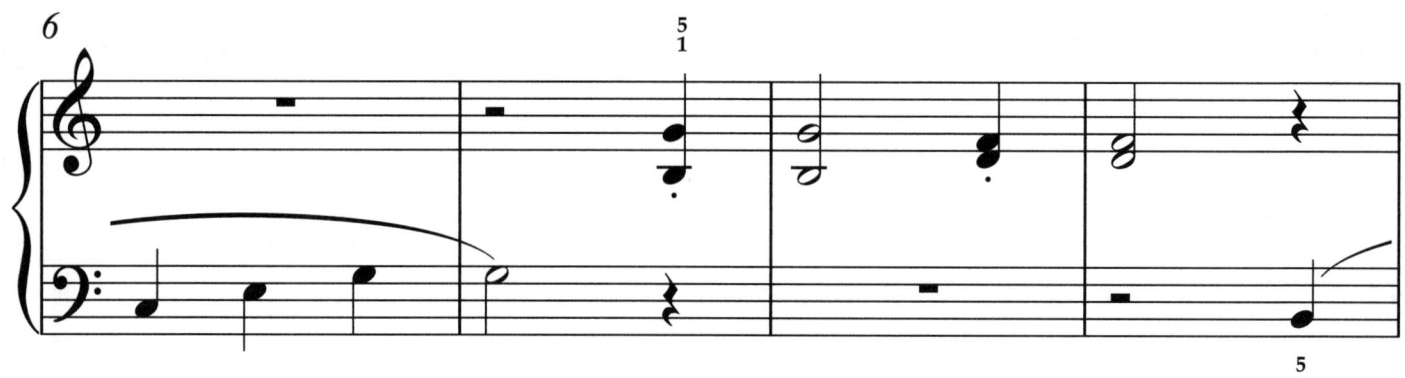
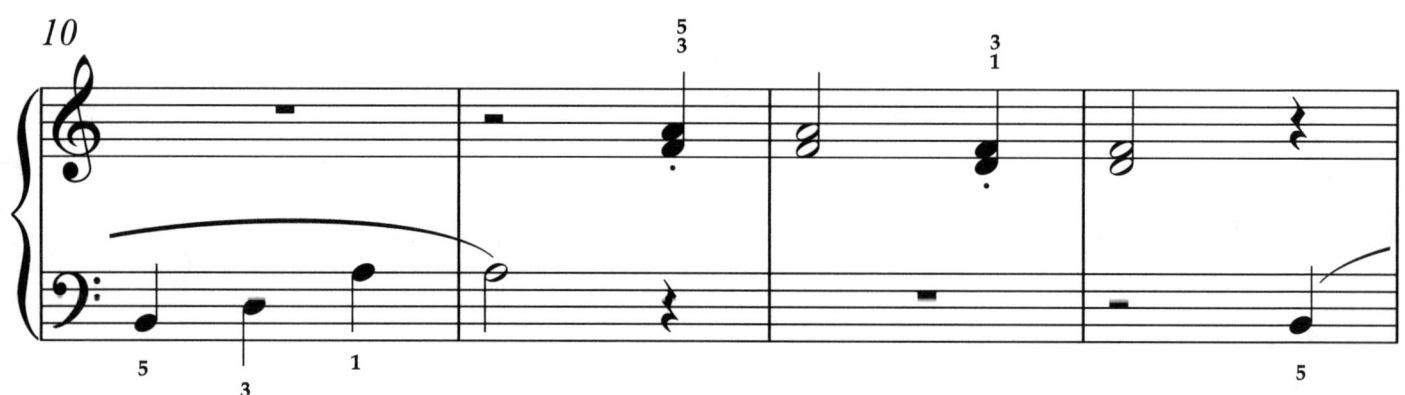
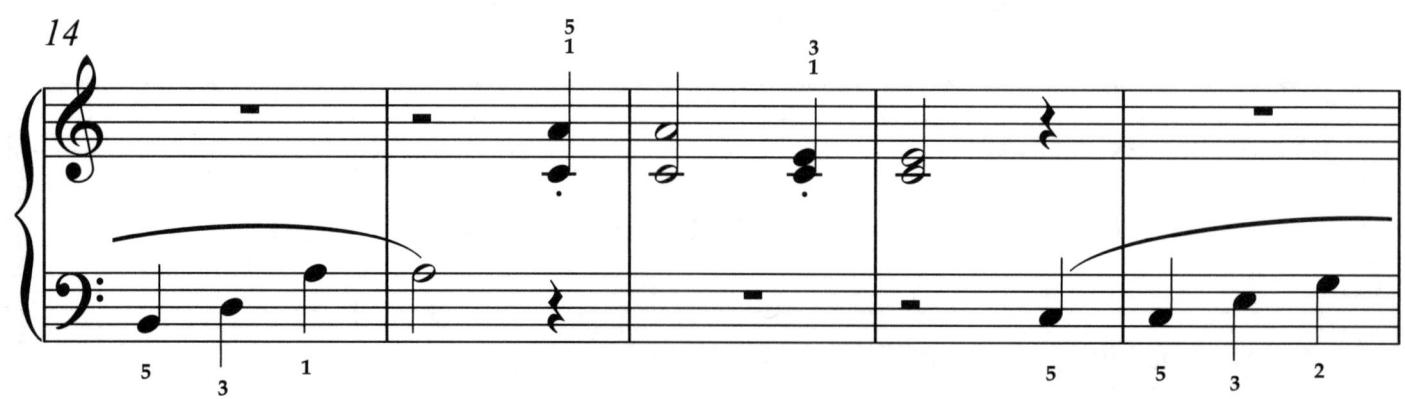

Copyright © 2006 Piano Pronto Publishing
PianoPronto.com

THE CLASSICAL PERIOD

(1750-1820)

There are four major periods in music history – Baroque, Classical, Romantic, and Contemporary. Let's learn some facts about the Classical period and the important composers who lived during this period.

IMPORTANT COMPOSERS

- **Franz Joseph Haydn** – (1732-1809)
- **Wolfgang Amadeus Mozart** – (1756-1791)
- **Ludwig van Beethoven** – (1770-1827)

MUSICAL STYLE OF THE CLASSICAL PERIOD

- Melodies were simple and symmetrical.
- The texture of compositions was primarily homophonic (melody and accompaniment)
- Many composers used folk melodies in their compositions.
- The structure of most Classical compositions consisted of simple two and three-part forms. Sonata allegro form was the primary structure used.

KEYBOARD MUSIC OF THE CLASSICAL PERIOD

- The piano was the primary keyboard instrument.
- Mozart composed 17 piano sonatas and 27 piano concertos. These pieces are standard literature for all pianists.
- Beethoven composed 32 piano sonatas. These works began pushing the limits of standard classical "forms" and harmonic structure. Beethoven offered a great amount of influence on the up and coming Romantic Period composers who continue down this same path.

PRONTO PREP

The next piece is a "*Mozart Medley*" which includes three famous melodies written by the great master. Play the examples below to help prepare for the next piece.

BEFORE YOU BEGIN:

- The first two pieces in the medley are in the *key of:* _____

- The last piece in the medley is in the *key of:* _____

Mozart Medley
"A Little Night Music" — Movement 2

W.A. Mozart
Arr. Jennifer Eklund

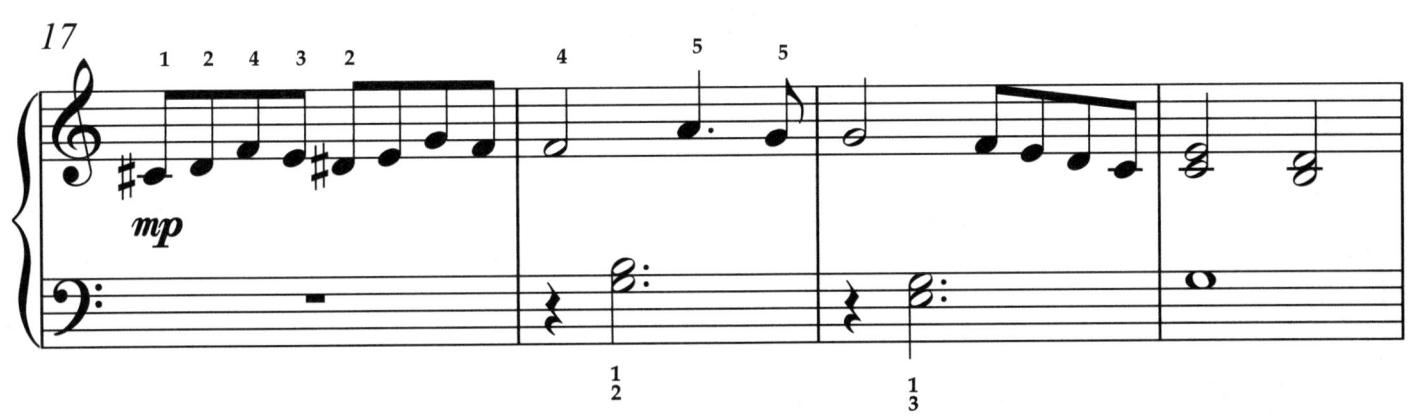

March of Welcome – from "Amadeus"

La ci darem la mano – from "Don Giovanni"

A MINOR REVIEW

Let's review some important facts about the key of A minor.

A Minor Scale (Natural Form)

Complete the scales on the staves below.

A Minor Key Signature

Draw the correct key signature below.

A minor is the relative minor of what major key? _____

A major key and its relative minor share the same _____

Which step of the major scales identifies the relative minor key? _____

There are _____ different forms of minor scales.

PRONTO PREP

Play the examples below to help prepare for "*Bourree.*"

BEFORE YOU BEGIN:

- *The composer of the next piece, **J.S. Bach**, composed during which period?*

       Baroque Period   or   **Classical Period**

- *Allegro* means _____.

Bourree

J.S. Bach
Arr. Jennifer Eklund

Allegro

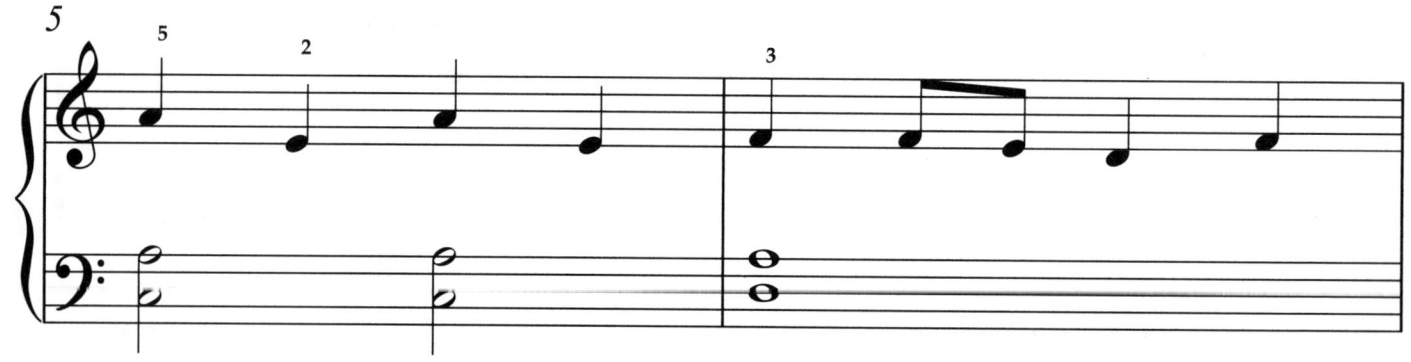

Copyright © 2006 Piano Pronto Publishing
PianoPronto.com

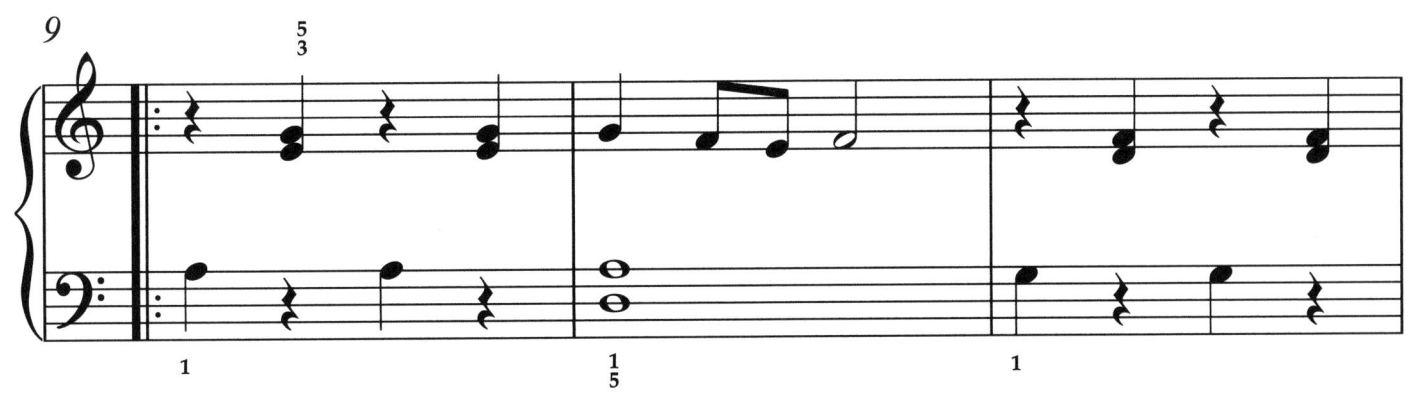

PRONTO PREP

Play the examples below to help prepare for "*Lullaby*."

BEFORE YOU BEGIN:

- The next piece is in the **key of**: _____

- What type of chord pattern is used in the bass clef?

Block chords   or   Broken chords

Lullaby

Johannes Brahms
Arr. Jennifer Eklund

Andante

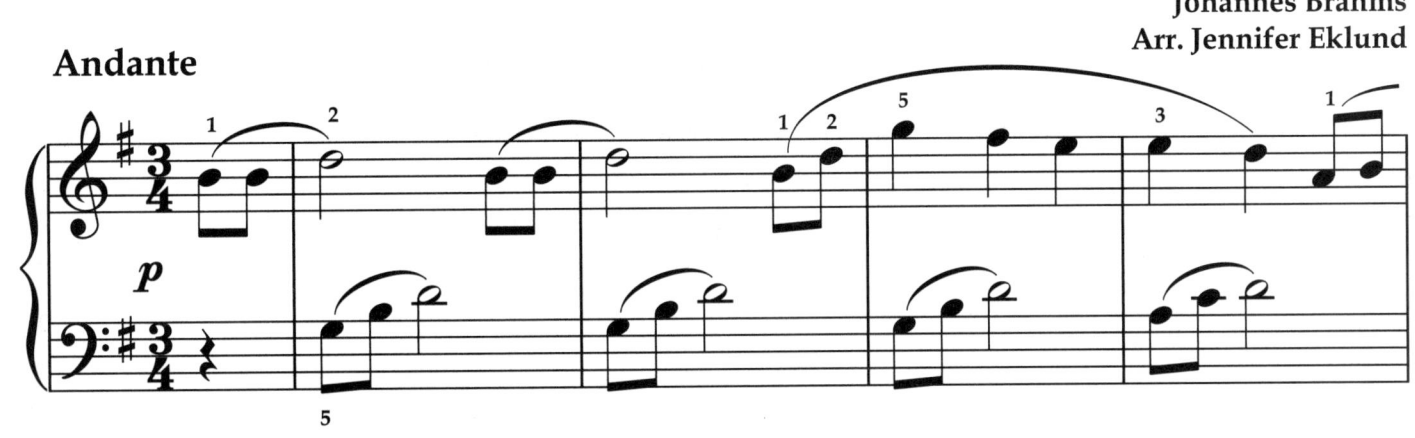

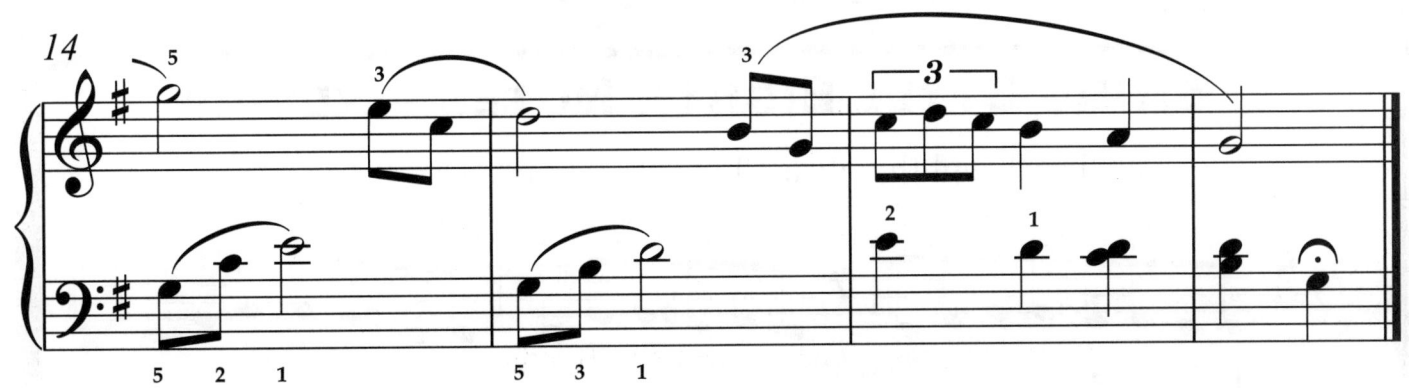

PRONTO PREP

Play the examples below to help prepare for "*Thursday Blues*."

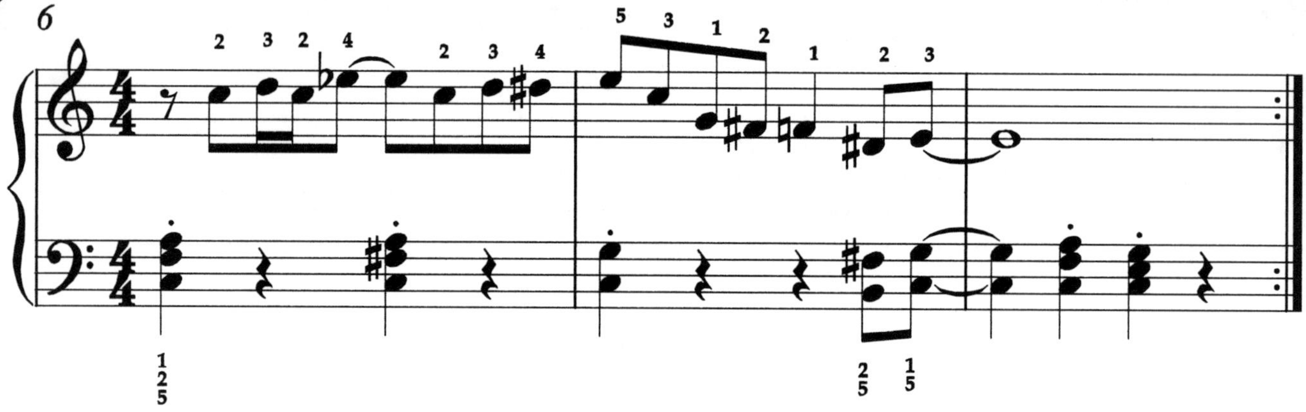

SWING STYLE EIGHTH NOTES – REVIEW

Label each eighth note as "long" or "short". Use "L" and "S".

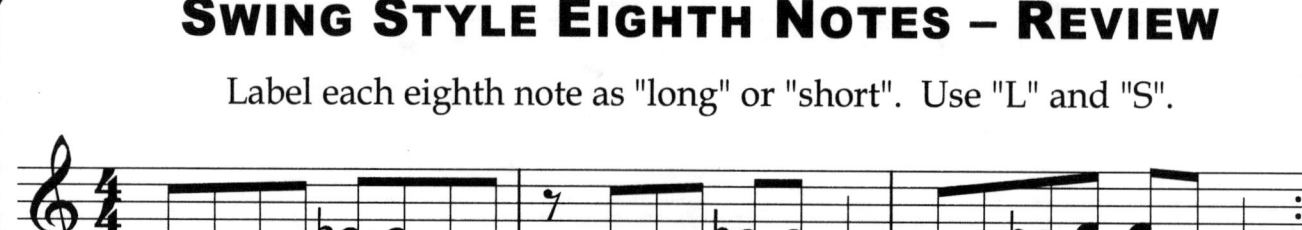

L S L S

Thursday Blues

Light & swinging

Jennifer Eklund

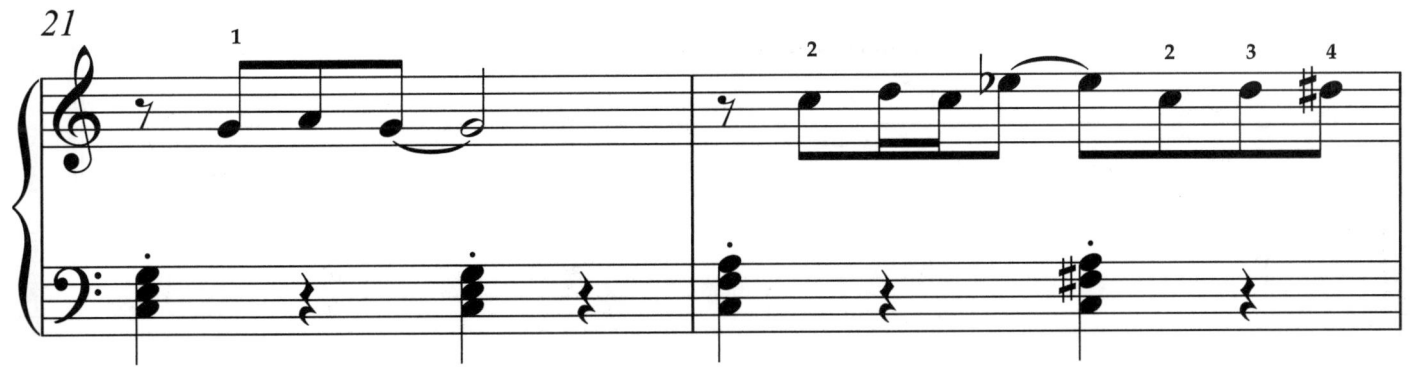

PRONTO PREP

Play the excerpts below to help prepare for "*Sakura*."

Sakura
(Cherry Blossoms)

Japanese Traditional
Arr. Jennifer Eklund

Moderately

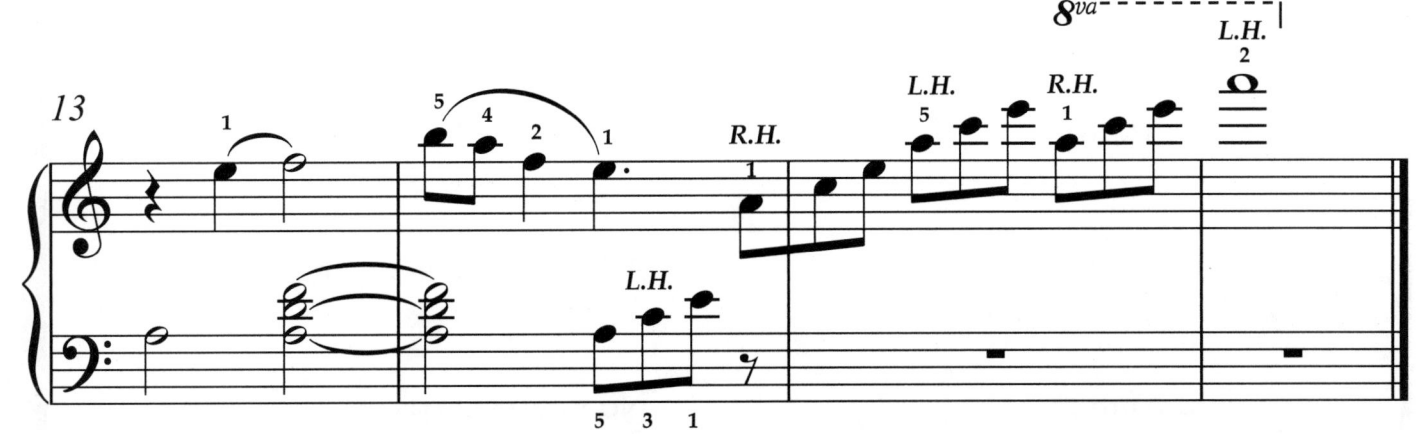

Copyright © 2006 Piano Pronto Publishing
PianoPronto.com

KEY SIGNATURE QUIZ

Key of: _____   Key of: _____   Key of: _____

Key of: _____   Key of: _____   Key of: _____

Matching

F Major   All F's are sharp

D Major   All B's are flat

C Major   All F's and C's are sharp

G Major   No flats/sharps

PRONTO PREP

Play the excerpts below to help prepare for "*Saint Anthony Chorale*."

BEFORE YOU BEGIN:

- The symbols in *measures 27-28* are called: **Accents**   or   **Fermatas**

- Label the **bass clef notes** in *measures 11-14*.

Saint Anthony Chorale

Joseph Haydn
Arr. Jennifer Eklund

Andante

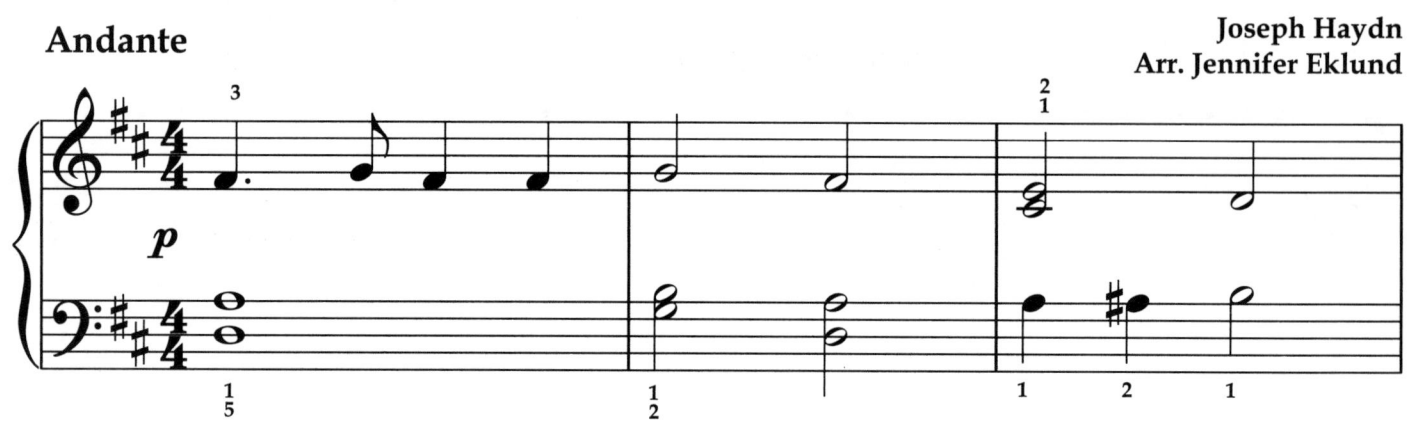
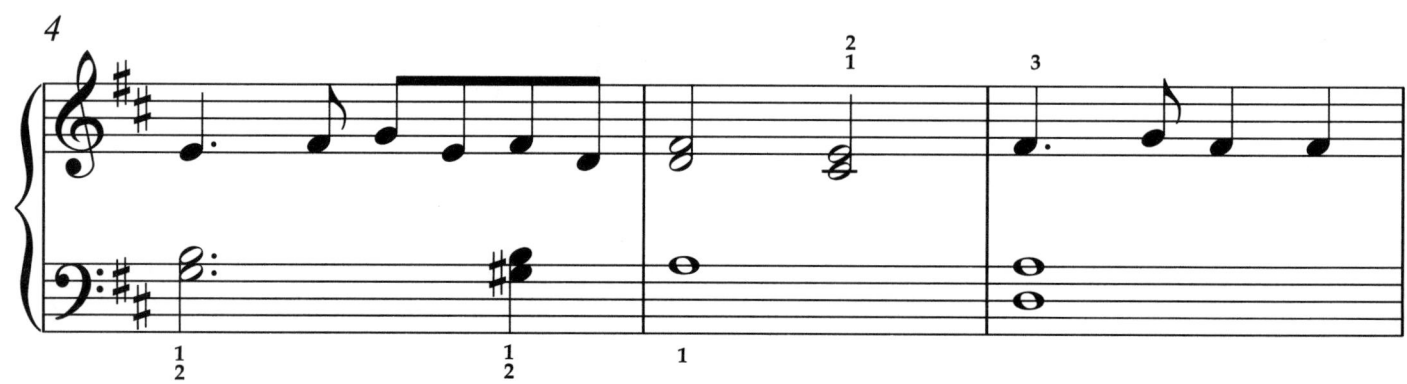

KEY OF D MINOR

D Minor Key Signature

All B's are flat.

D Minor Scale (Natural Minor)

Practice playing the D minor scale in each hand. Watch the fingerings!

Who is my Relative?

 AND

_____ Major   D Minor

PRONTO PREP

Play the examples below to help prepare for "*In the Hall of the Mountain King.*"

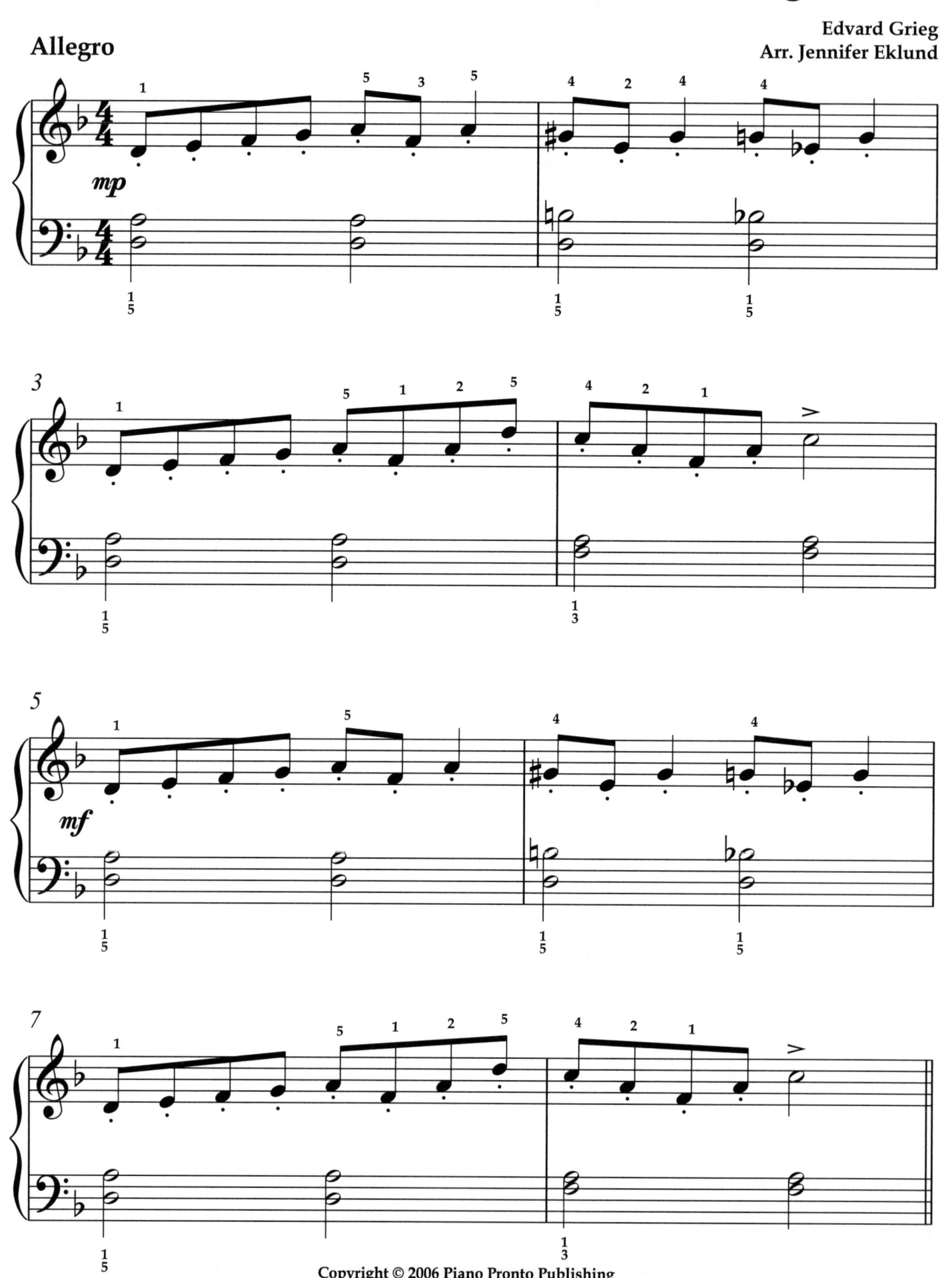

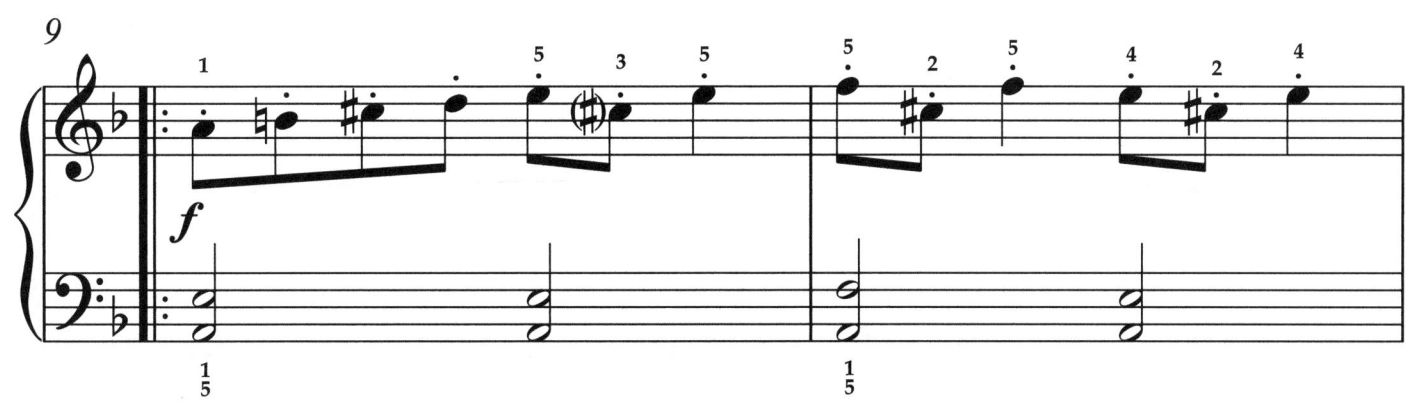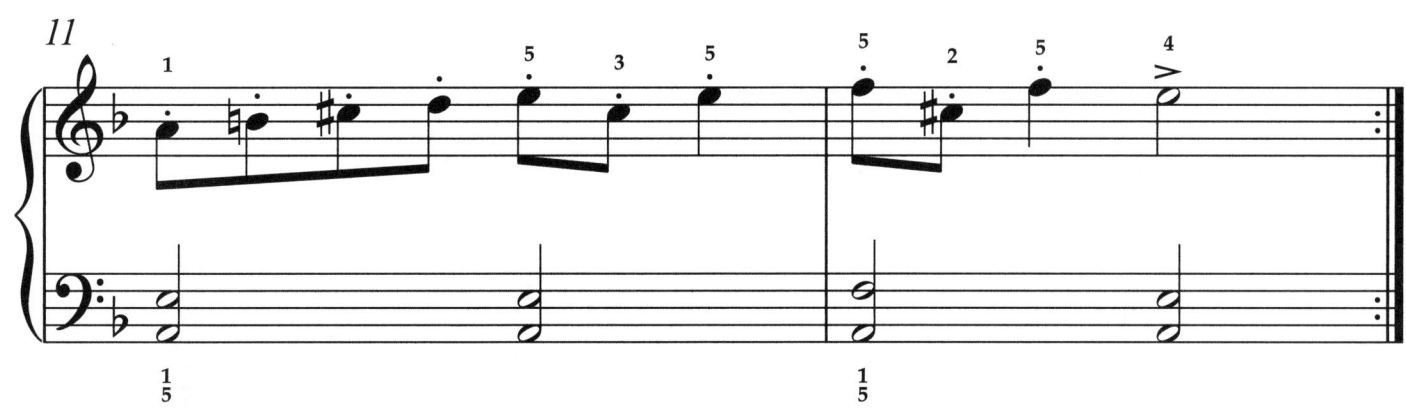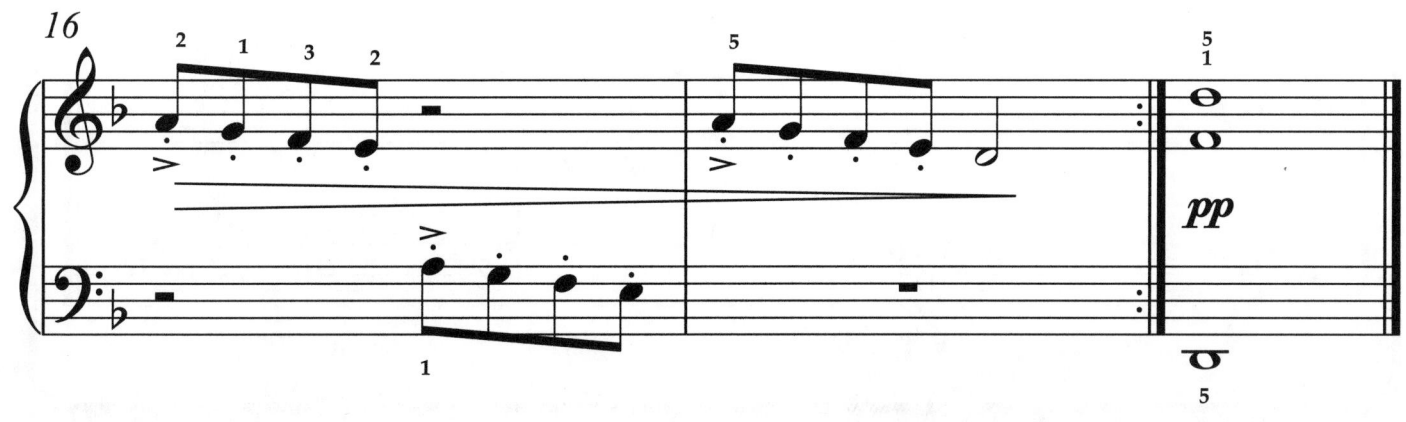

PRONTO PREP

Play the examples below to help prepare for "*Chopin Medley*."

NEW TEMPO MARKING

Lento   =   Slow, slightly faster than *largo*.

TEMPO REVIEW

Andante _____

Allegro _____

Largo _____

Moderato _____

Lento _____

Allegretto _____

BEFORE YOU BEGIN:

- The **time signature** of the first piece in the medley is: _____

- The **time signature** of the second piece in the medley is: _____

- Label the **treble clef notes** in **measure 20**.

- Label the **bass clef notes** in **measures 22 and 23**.

Chopin Medley
Etude Theme

Frederic Chopin
Arr. Jennifer Eklund

Nocturne Theme

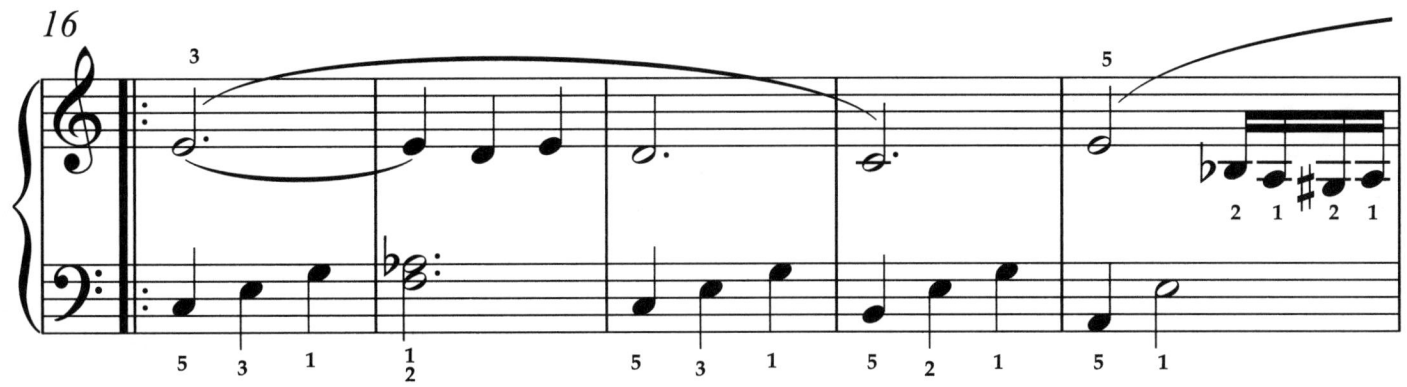

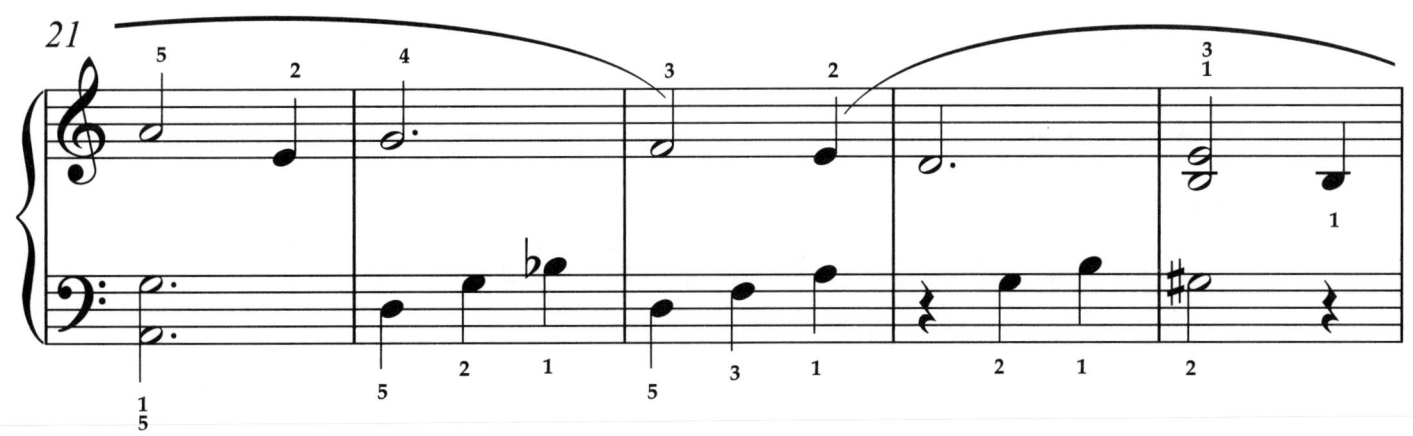

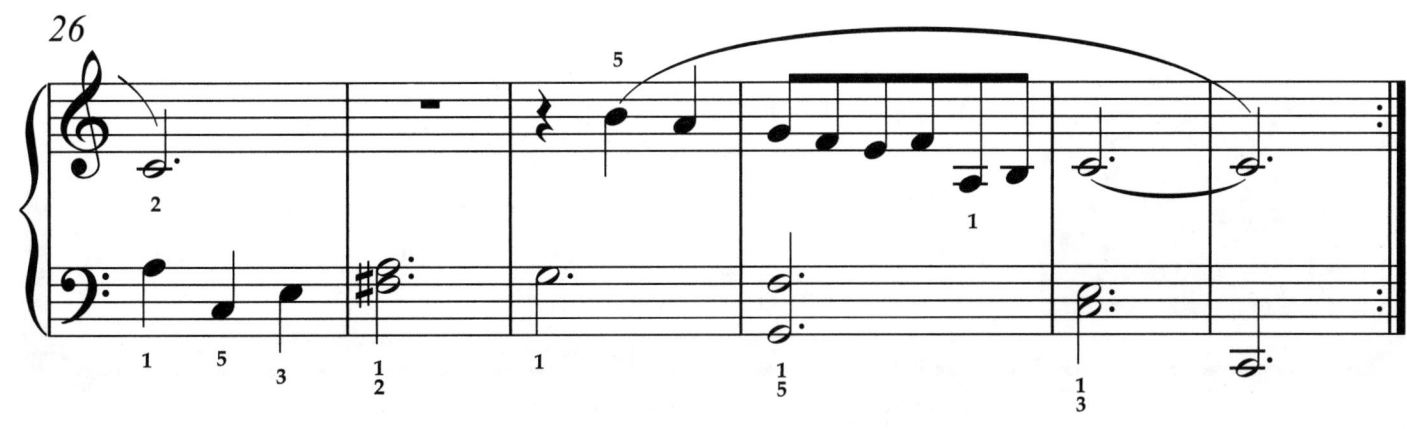

RAGTIME MUSIC

Ragtime music is a style of American music which originated in the late 1800s. Let's learn some important facts about this style of music.

RAGTIME STYLE

- Ragtime music originated in African American communities in the 1890s.
- The key element of ragtime music is the use of *syncopation*. Syncopated rhythm uses accents on weak beats. Look at the example below:

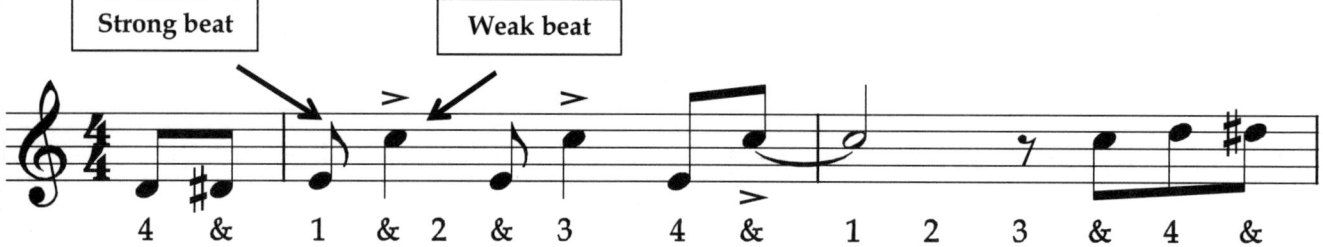

- The use of this "ragged" rhythmic style is believed to be the origin of the word "ragtime."
- Ragtime music was written primarily for the piano.
- The ragtime era officially ended in the early 1920s when jazz became popular.
- Ragtime is considered to be a form of "classical music" by many historians because ragtime compositions were written down and not improvised like jazz

SCOTT JOPLIN – KING OF RAGTIME MUSIC

The first ragtime piece you will learn, "***The Entertainer***," was written by a famous ragtime composer named Scott Joplin. Here are some important facts about him.

- Joplin was classically trained by a German teacher who taught him about European "classical" forms.
- After publishing "***Maple Leaf Rag***" in 1899, Joplin became the most prominent ragtime performer in the country. He received a royalty of one penny for each copy of his sheet music that sold.
- His many compositions elevated the ragtime genre to a respected and serious art form.

PRONTO PREP

Play the examples below to help prepare for "*The Entertainer.*"

The Entertainer

Allegretto

Scott Joplin
Arr. Jennifer Eklund

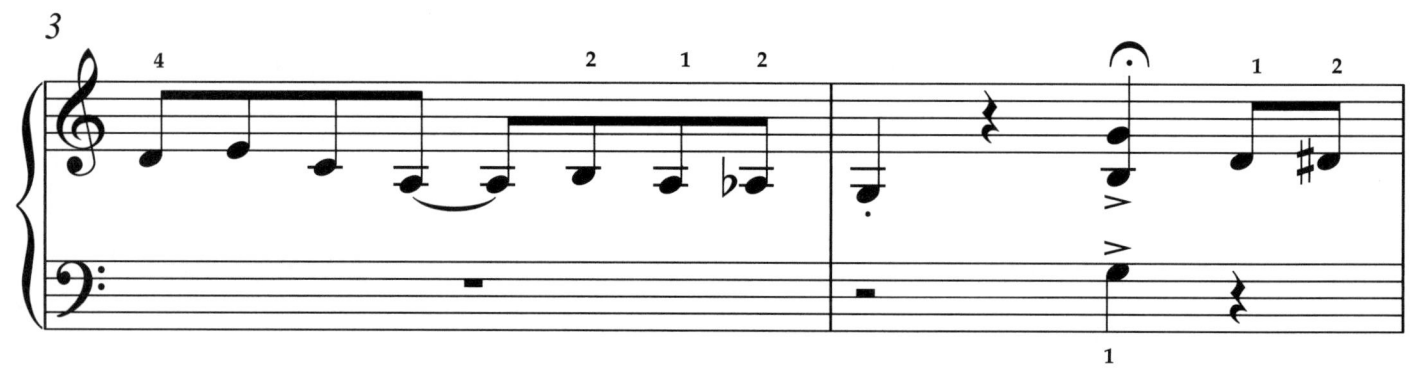

Copyright © 2006 Piano Pronto Publishing
PianoPronto.com

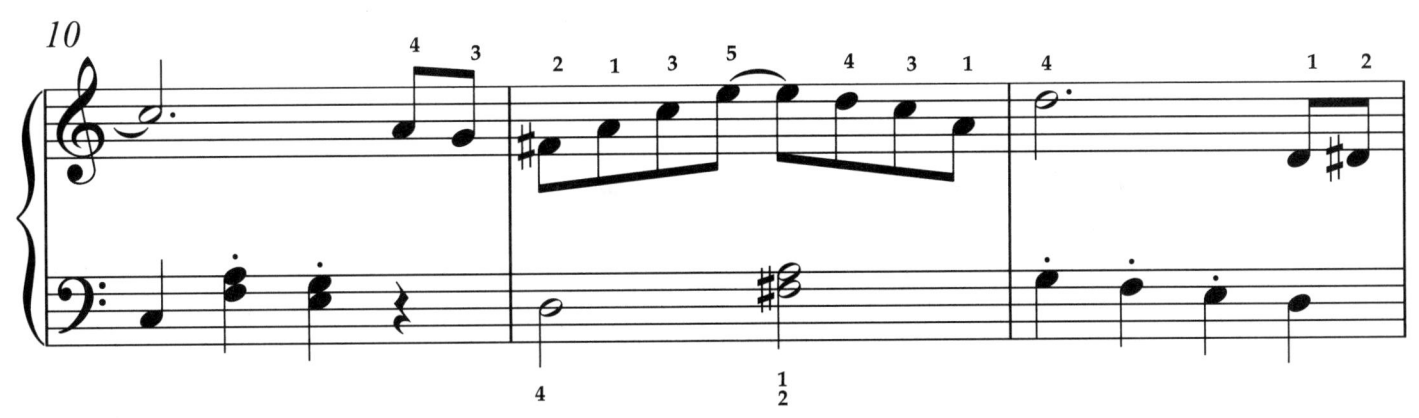

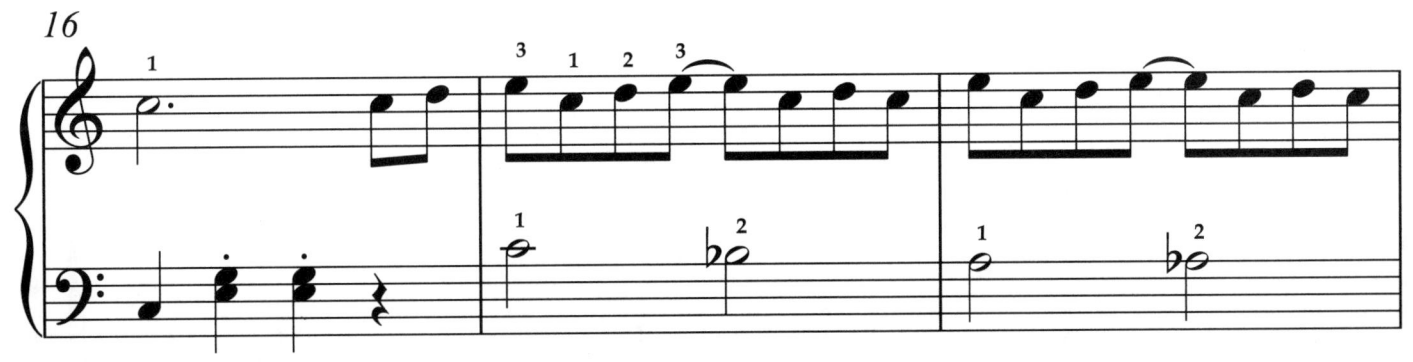

PRONTO PREP

Play the examples below to help prepare for "*Medley of Vocal Classics.*"

BEFORE YOU BEGIN:

- *The first piece in the medley is in the **key of**:* _____

- *The second piece in the medley is in the **key of**:* _____

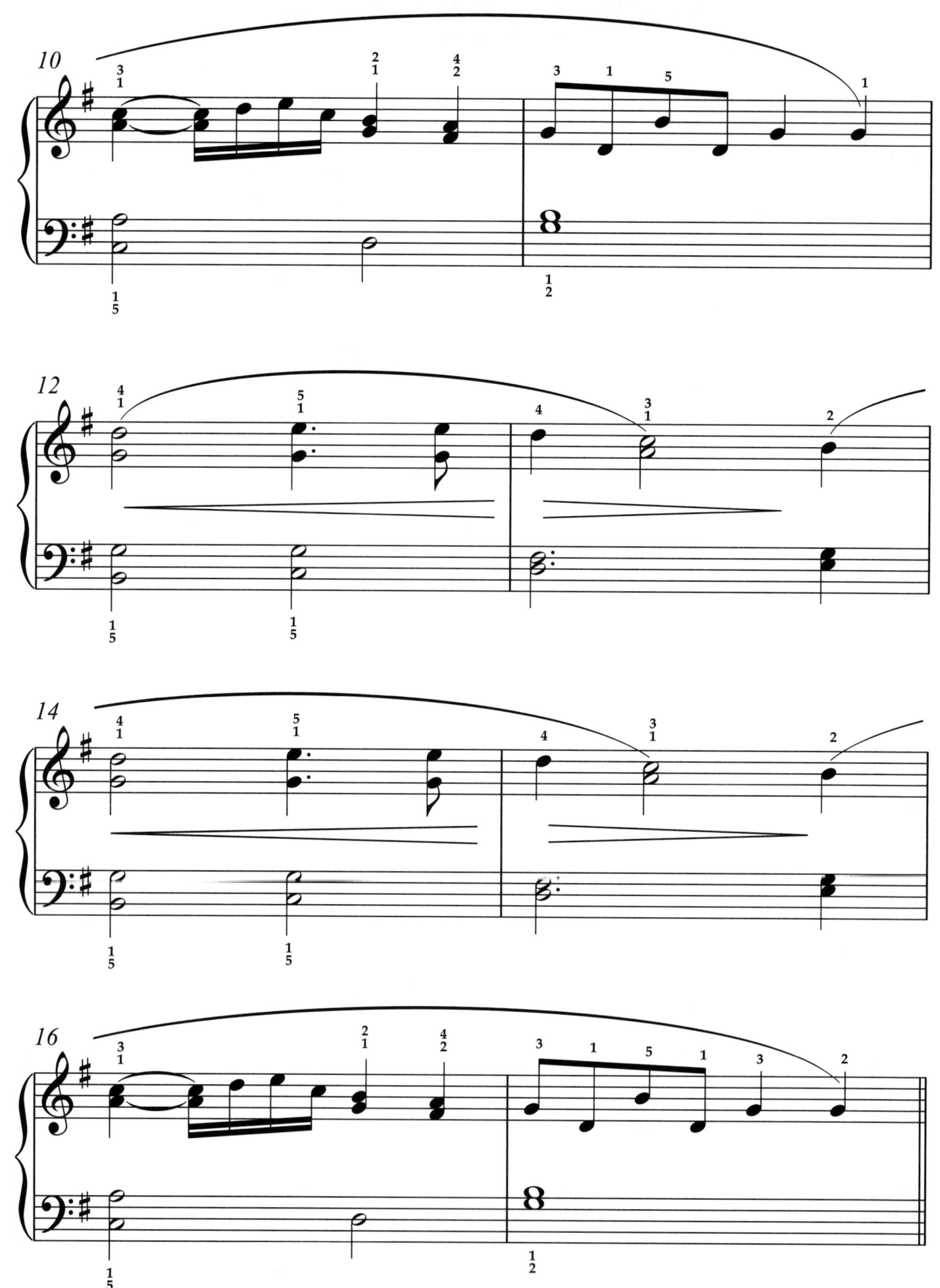

Caro mio ben
(Thou all my bliss)

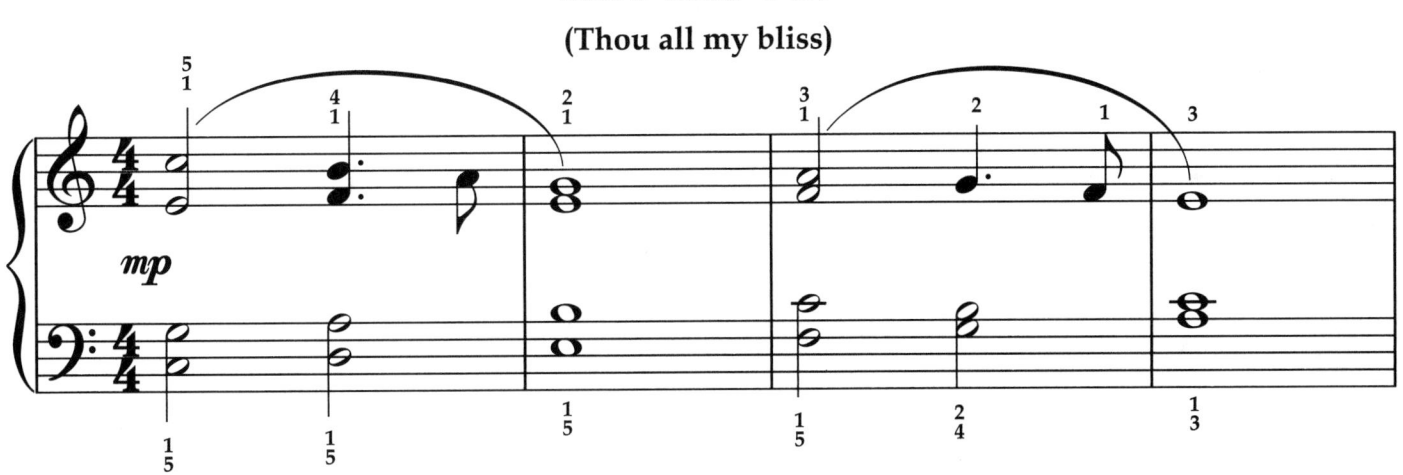
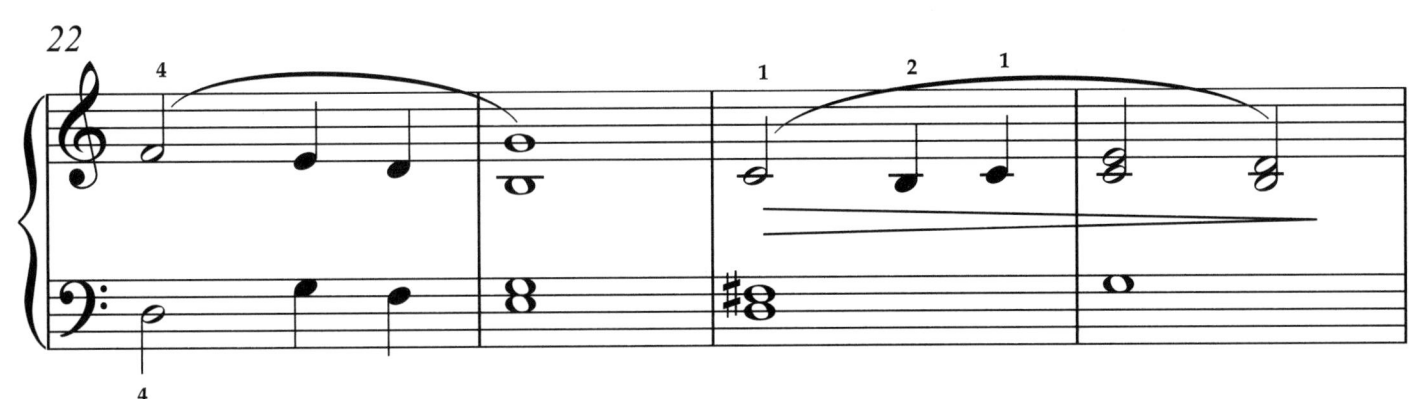
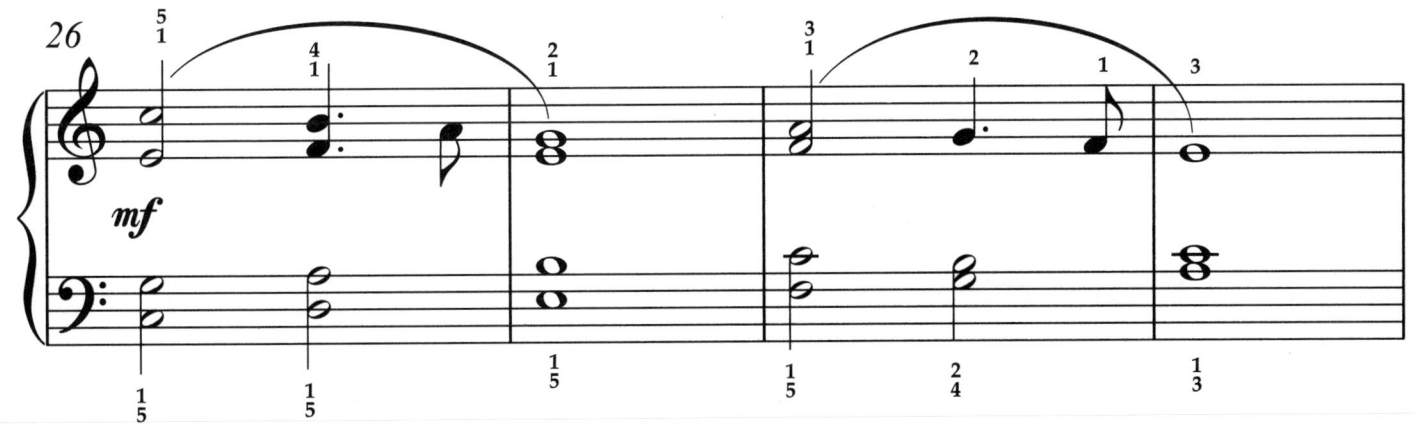

PRONTO PREP

Play the examples below to help prepare for "*Spring Theme #3.*"

BEFORE YOU BEGIN:

- The next piece is in the **key of**: _____

- In the key of _____ all _____ and _____ are _____.

Spring Theme #3

Antonio Vivaldi
Arr. Jennifer Eklund

Allegro

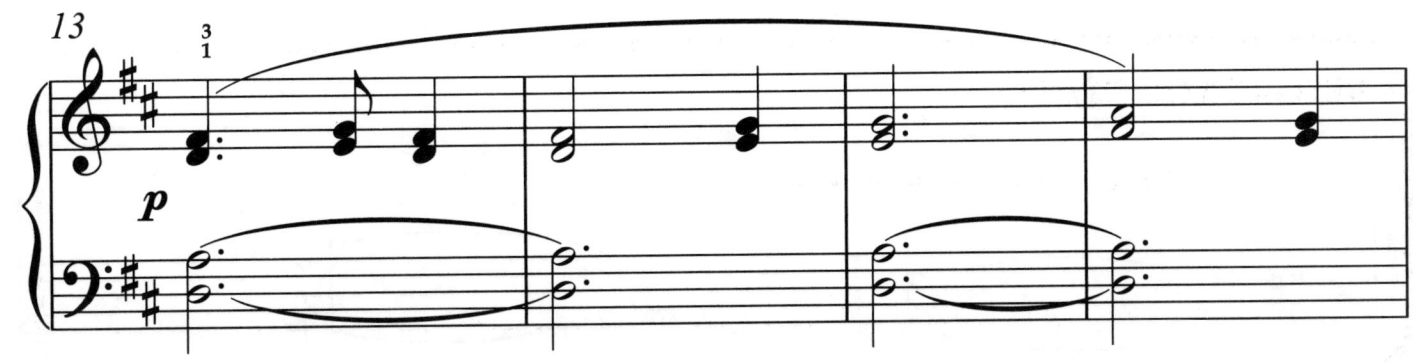

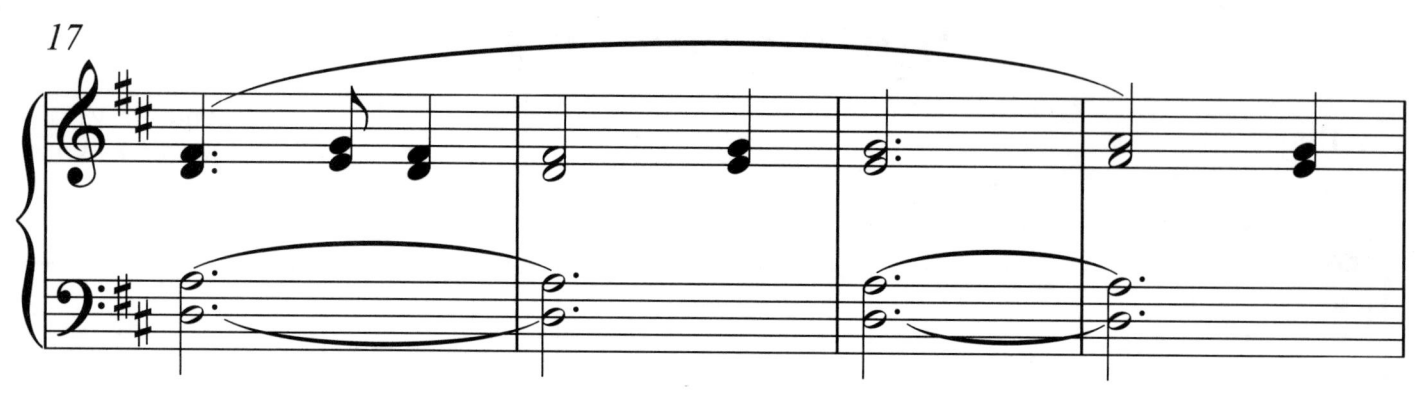

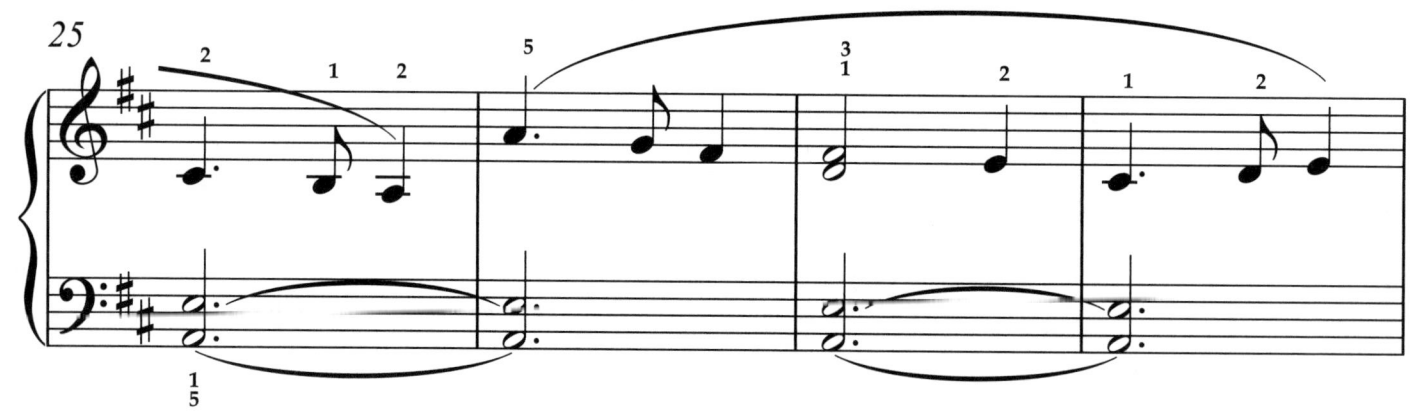
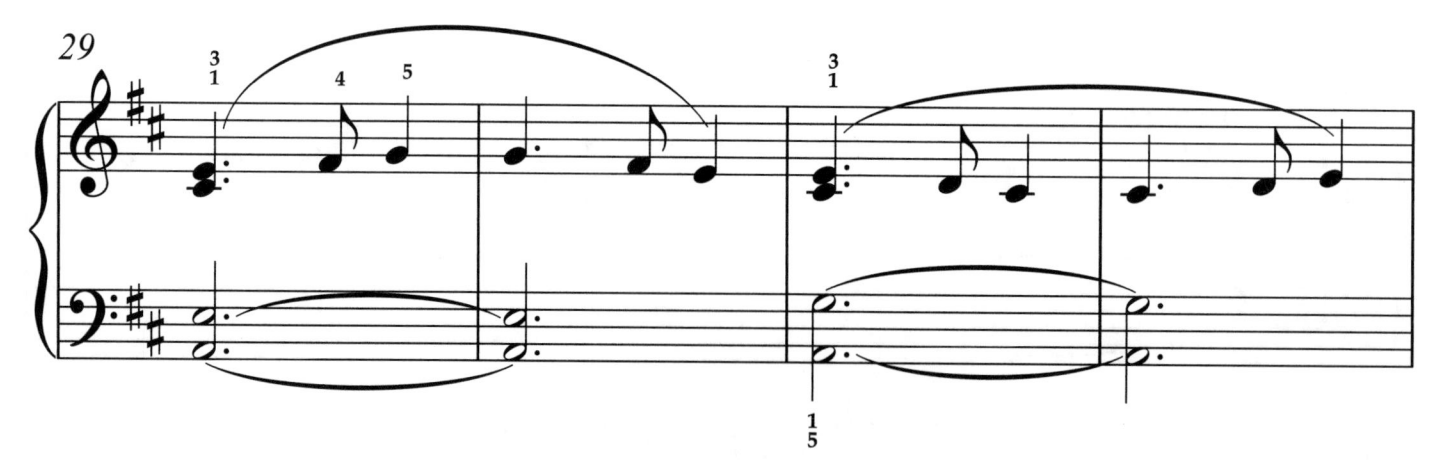

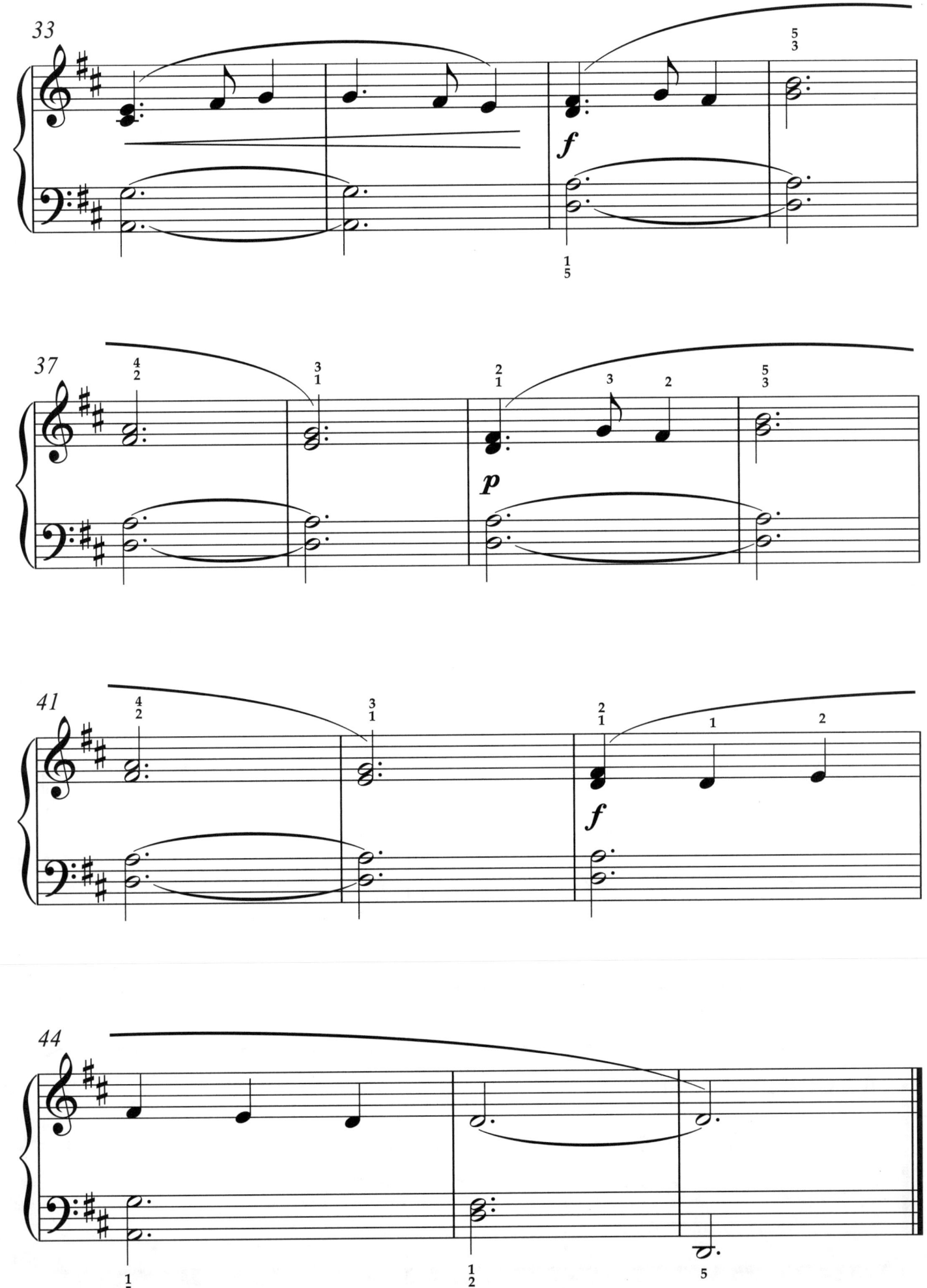

PRONTO PREP

Play the examples below to help prepare for "*Liebestraum*."

BEFORE YOU BEGIN:

- At **measure 26** what type of chords are used?   **Block**   or   **Broken**

- *Andante* means _____.

Liebestraum
(Dream of Love)

Franz Liszt
Arr. Jennifer Eklund

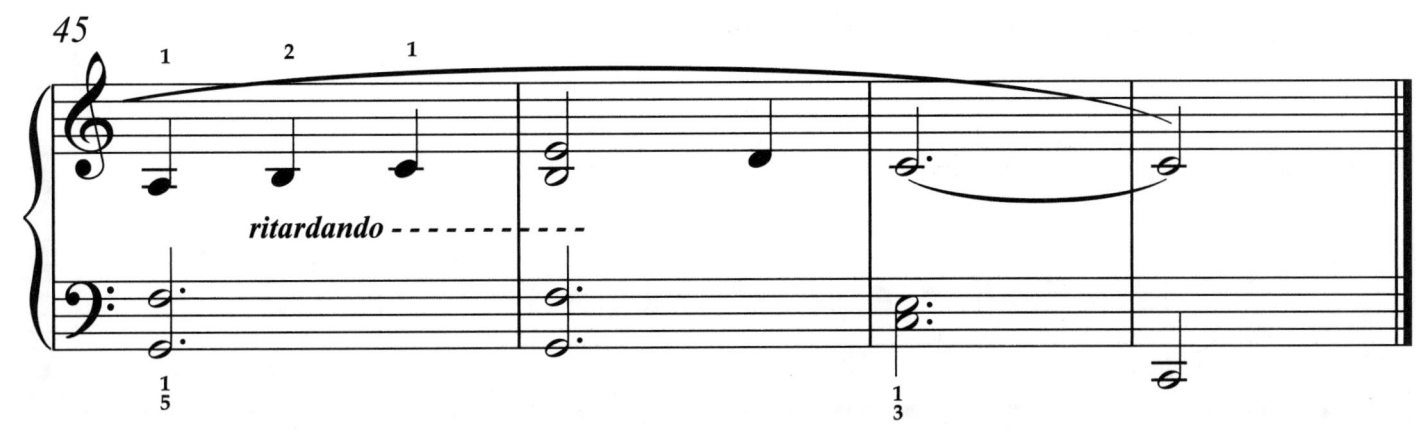

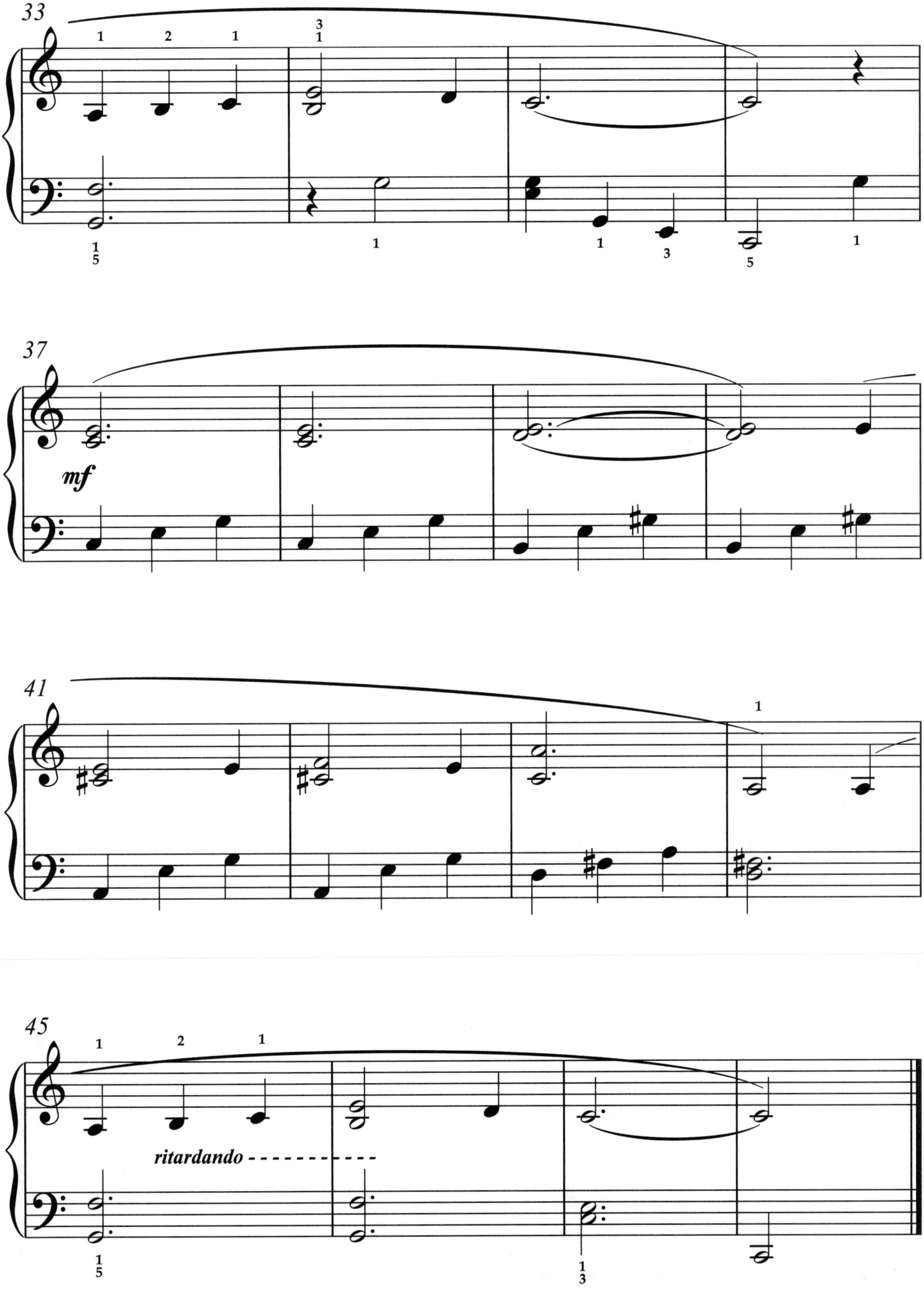
33
37
mf
41
45
ritardando

B♭ MAJOR

B♭ Major Key Signature

All B's and E's are flat.

B♭ Major Scale

Practice playing the B♭ major scale in each hand. Watch the fingerings!

Pronto Prep

Play the examples below to help prepare for "*Italian Air*."

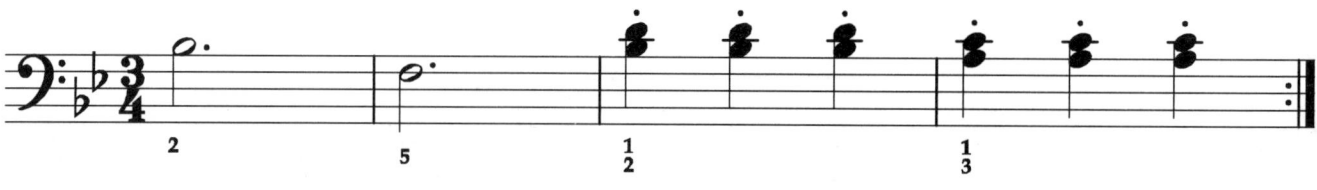

Italian Air

Traditional
Arr. Jennifer Eklund

Lightly

PRONTO PREP

Play the examples below to help prepare for "**Blues Medley**." Play all of the eighth notes in swing style, i.e. *"long, short, long, short"*.

Blues Medley
He's Got The Whole World In His Hands

Traditional
Arr. Jennifer Eklund

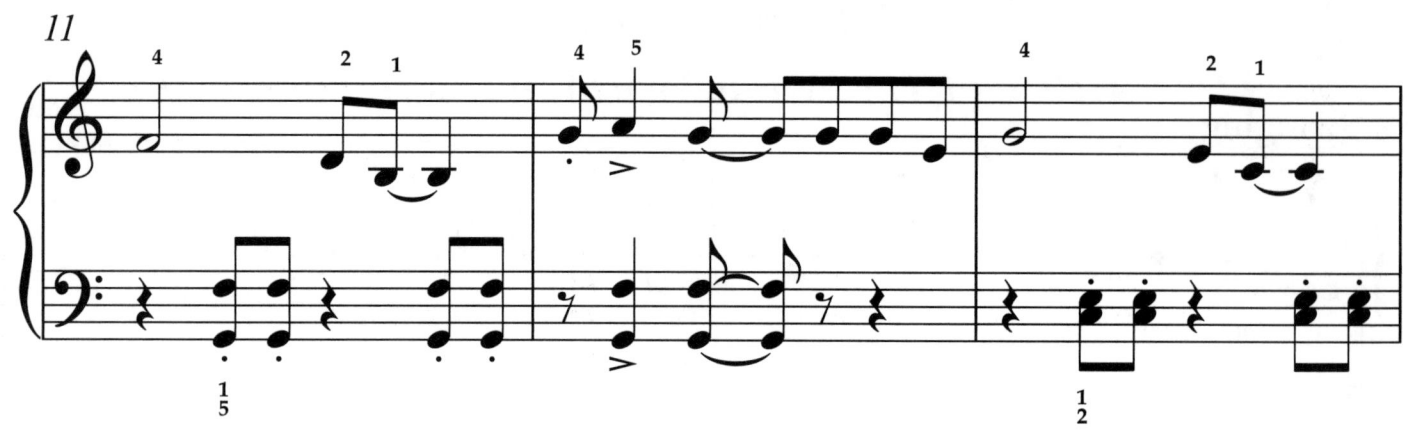

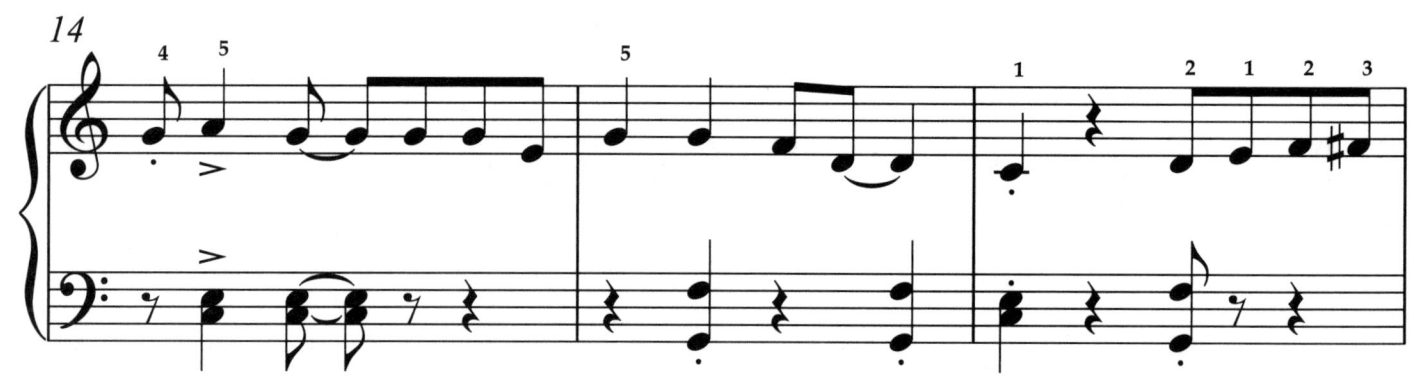

Cotton Mill Blues

* Alternate "shake" these notes as fast as you can!

PRONTO PREP

Play the examples below to help prepare for "*The Arkansas Traveler.*"

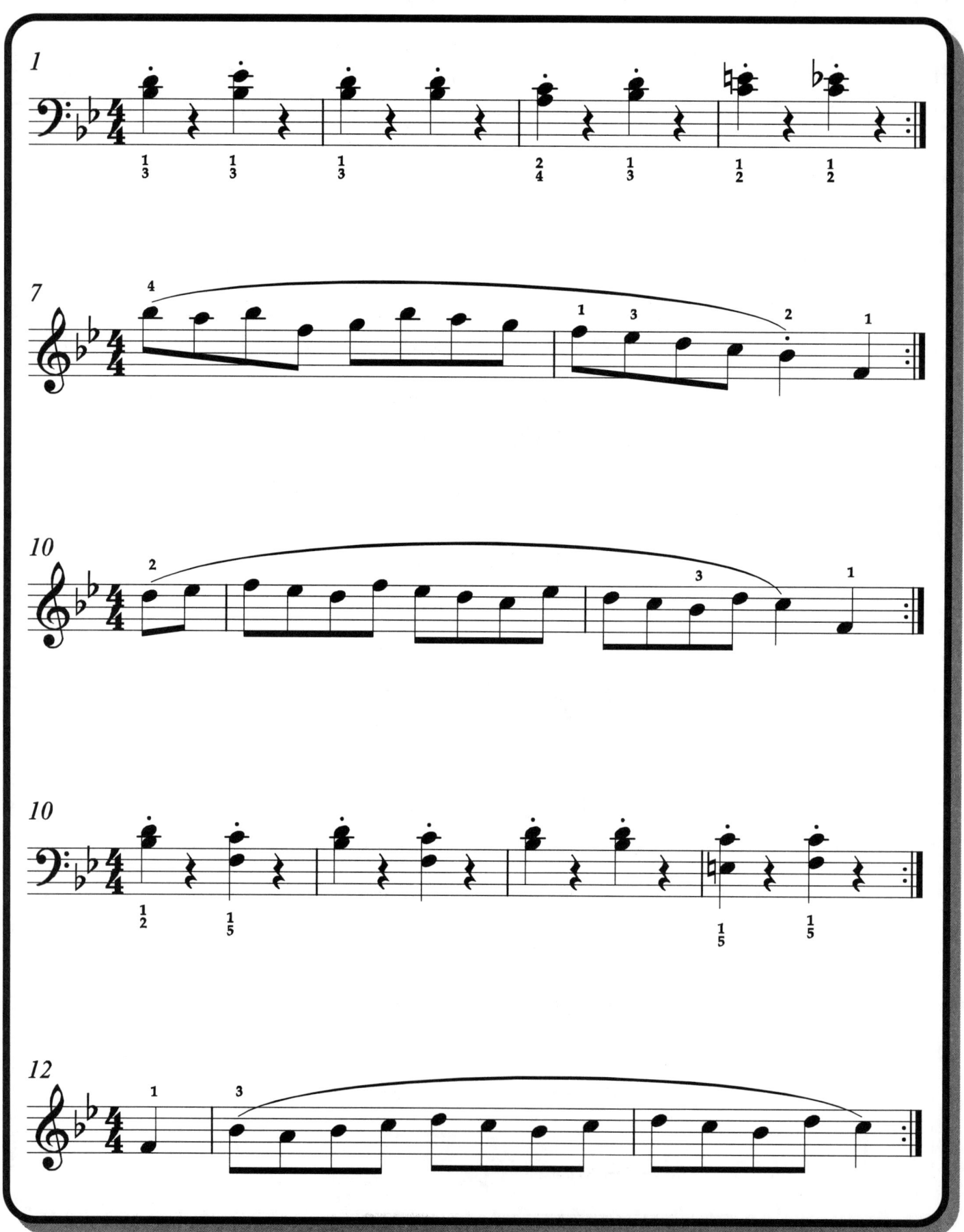

B♭ MAJOR REVIEW

B♭ MAJOR SCALE

Draw the B♭ major scale on the staves below

B♭ MAJOR KEY SIGNATURE

Draw the B♭ major key signature on the empty grand staff below.

In the key of B♭ major, all _____ and _____ are _____.

BEFORE YOU BEGIN:

- Label the **bass clef notes** in **measures 3 and 4**.

- What **articulation** is used in the **bass clef**?　　Accents　　or　　Staccato

- Explain the **ending system**.

The Arkansas Traveler

Traditional
Arr. Jennifer Eklund

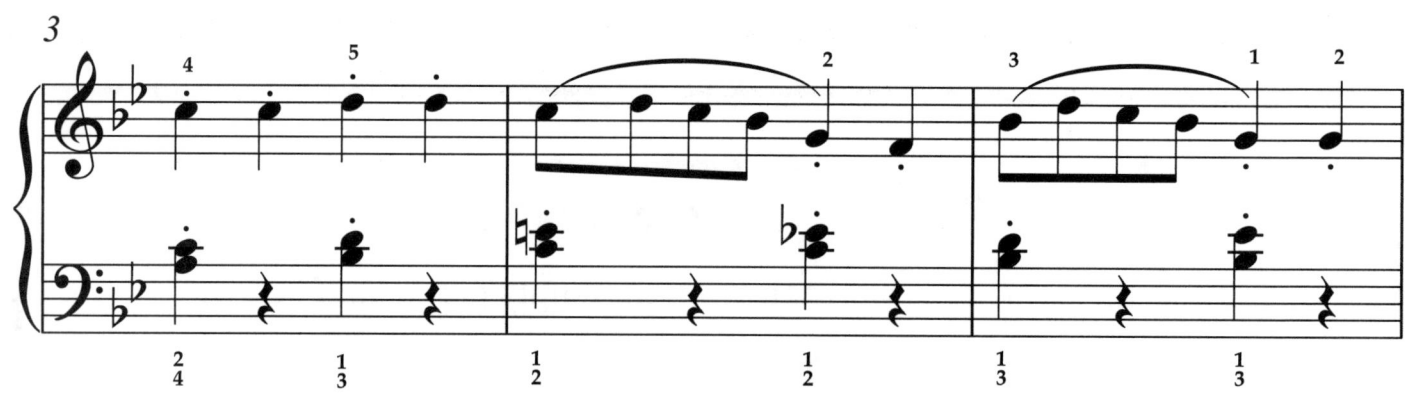
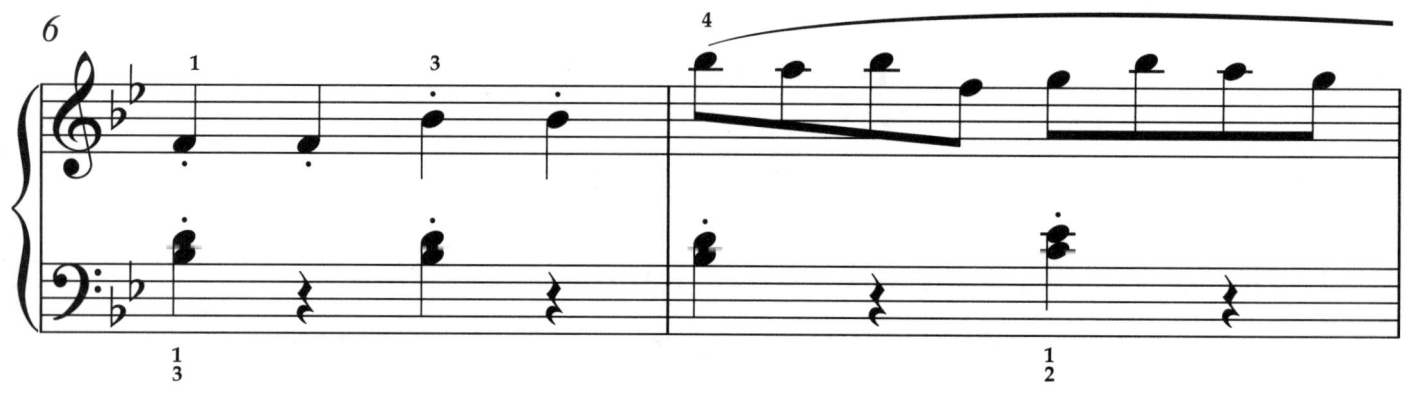
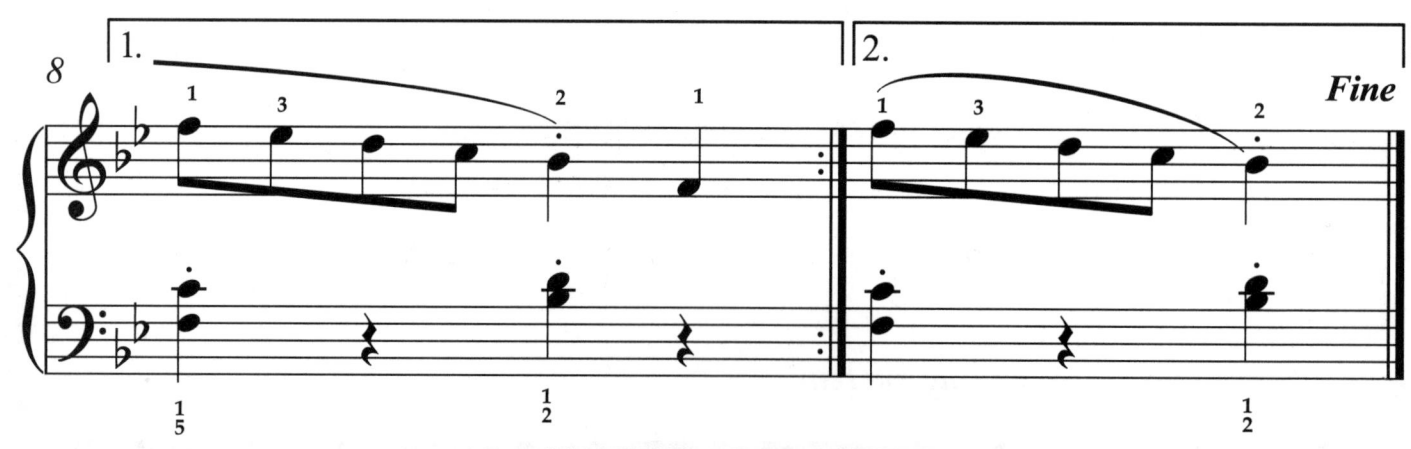

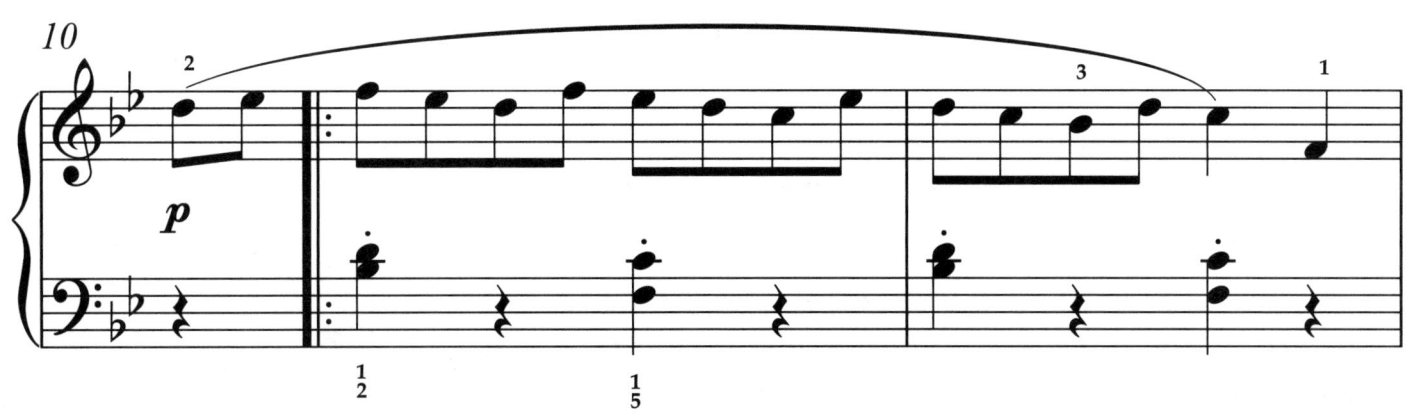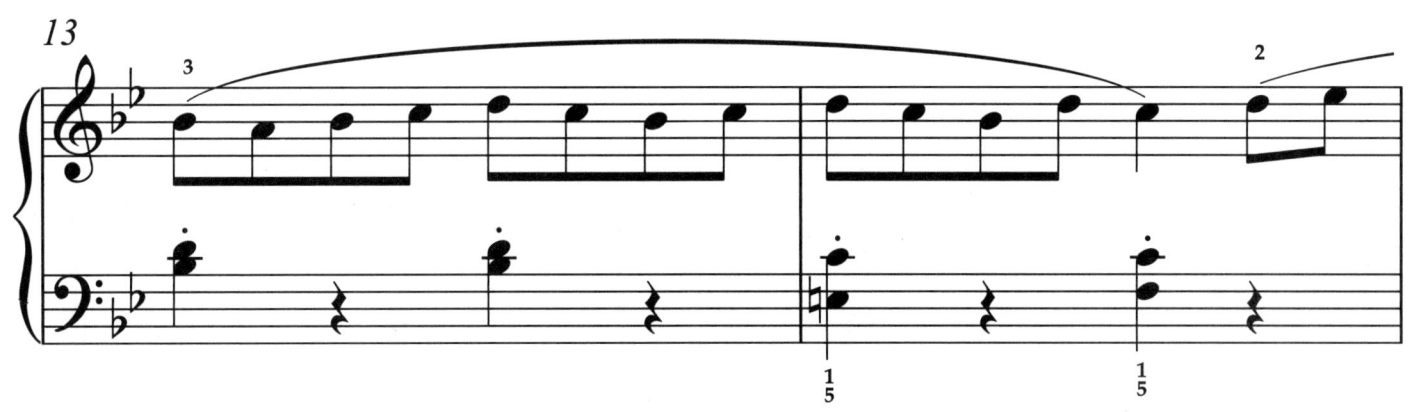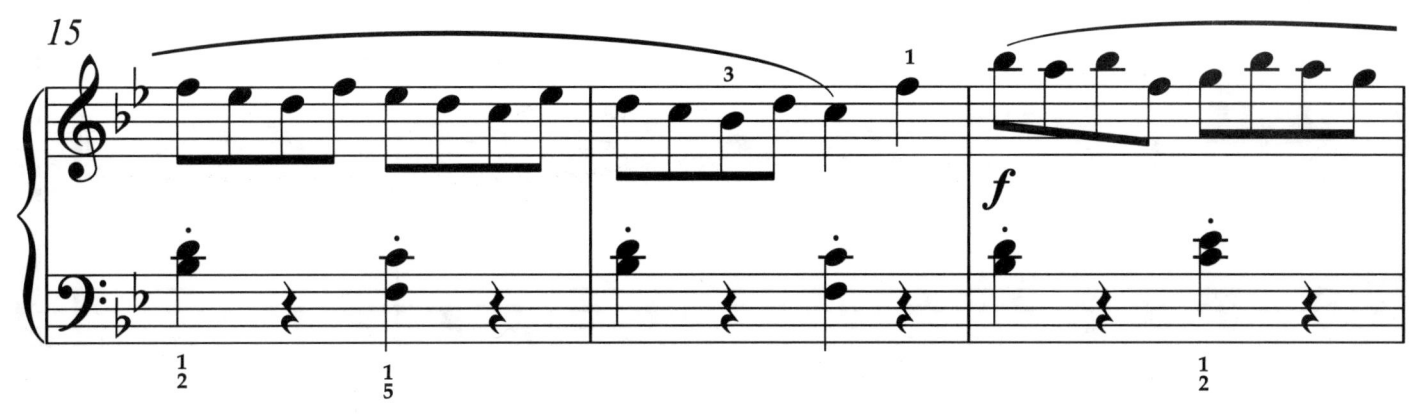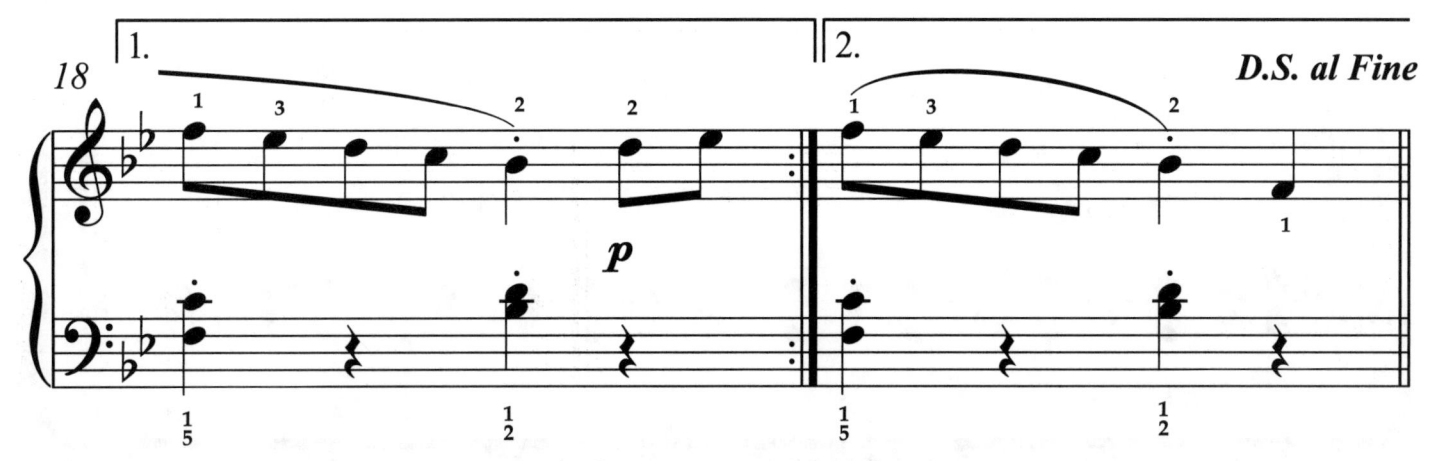

PRONTO PREP

Play the examples below to help prepare for "*Hungarian Rhapsody #2.*"

NEW TEMPO

Presto = Very fast.

NEW TERM

accelerando = Getting faster.
(can be abbreviated as *accel.*)

DRAW THE SYMBOL

Draw the correct symbol next to each term.

Play loud   _____

Play medium soft   _____

Play soft   _____

Gradually louder   _____

Gradually softer   _____

Getting slower   _____

Play medium loud   _____

Getting faster   _____

Hungarian Rhapsody #2

Franz Liszt
Arr. Jennifer Eklund

KEY OF G MINOR

G Minor Key Signature

All B's and E's are flat.

G Minor Scale (Natural Minor)

Practice playing the G minor scale in each hand. Watch the fingerings!

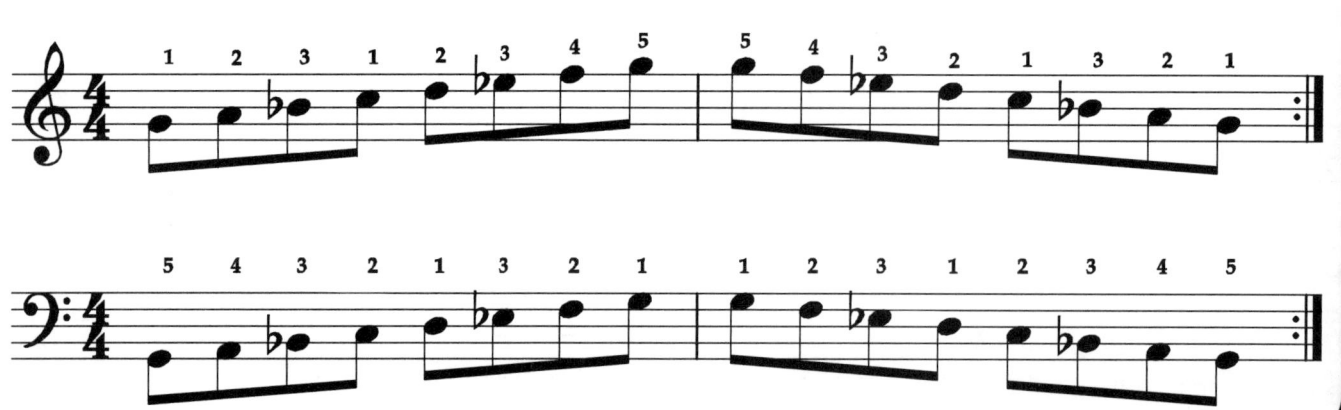

Who is my Relative?

 AND

_____ Major   G Minor

NEW TERM

a tempo = At the original tempo

PRONTO PREP

Play the examples below to help prepare for "*Swan Lake.*"

Swan Lake

Tchaikovsky
Arr. Jennifer Eklund

Andante

WHAT IS A PHRASE?

A phrase is a musical thought or idea. Slurs often define where the phrases are in a piece of music. We use the word phrasing to describe how to play a musical idea. The next piece will use a common type of phrasing called a two note slur.

TWO-NOTE SLURS

Look at the example below to learn how to properly play this articulation.

DROP AND LIFT

To properly play a two note slur your wrist needs to drop slightly when you strike the first note, and lift slightly when you strike the second note. Try playing the example below.

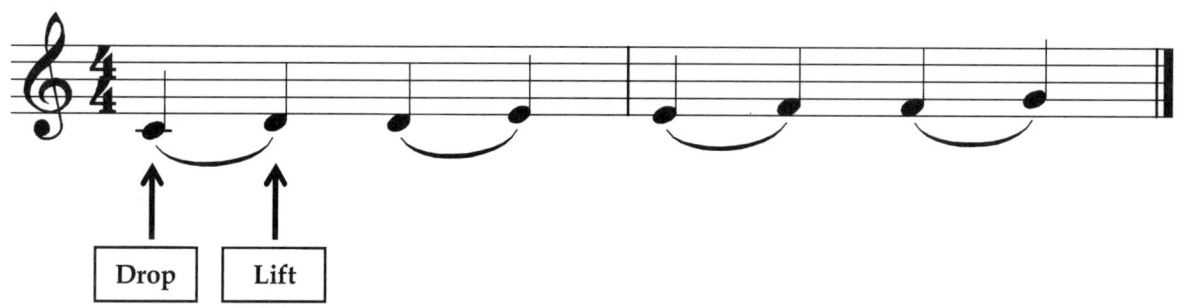

NOW IT'S YOUR TURN

Play the examples below to practice two-note slurs in each hand.

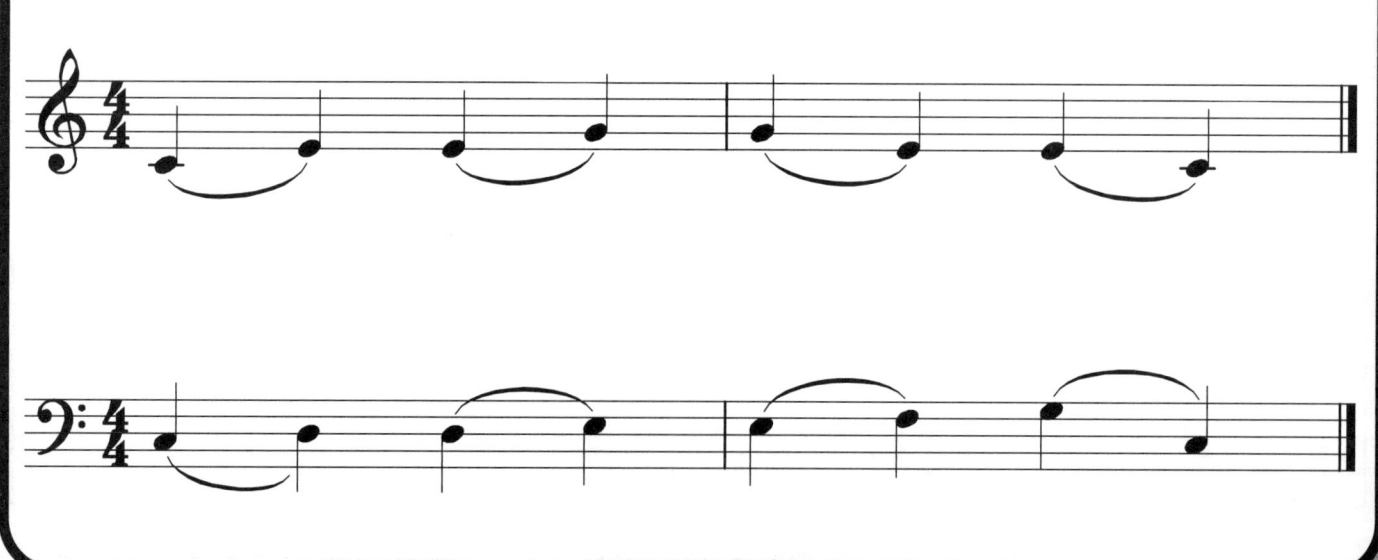

PRONTO PREP

Play the examples below to help prepare for "*Dance of the Hours*."

Dance of the Hours

Amilcare Ponchielli
Arr. Jennifer Eklund

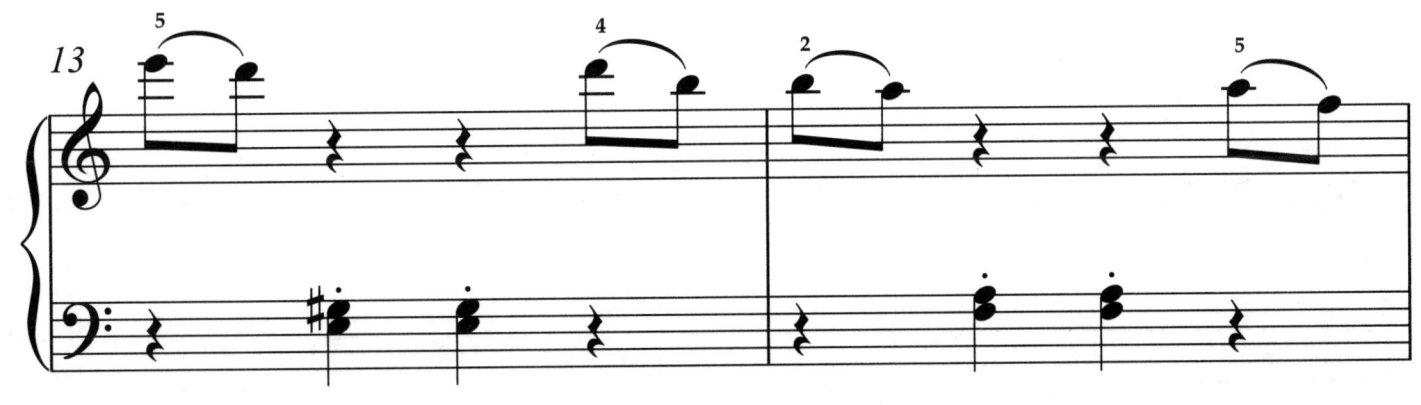

PRONTO PREP

Play the examples below to help prepare for "*Medley of Italian Songs*."

Medley of Italian Songs
O Sole Mio

Capua/Cottrau
Arr. Jennifer Eklund

Andante

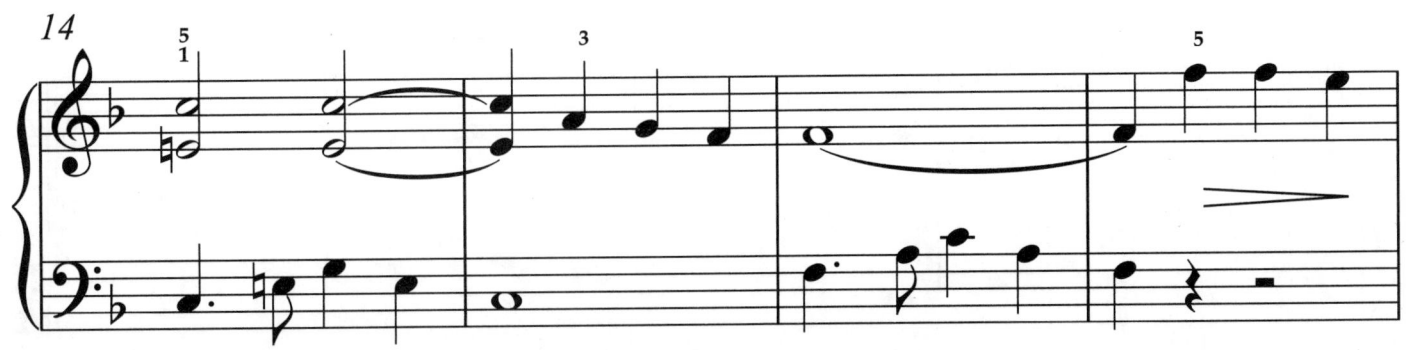

Copyright © 2006 Piano Pronto Publishing
PianoPronto.com

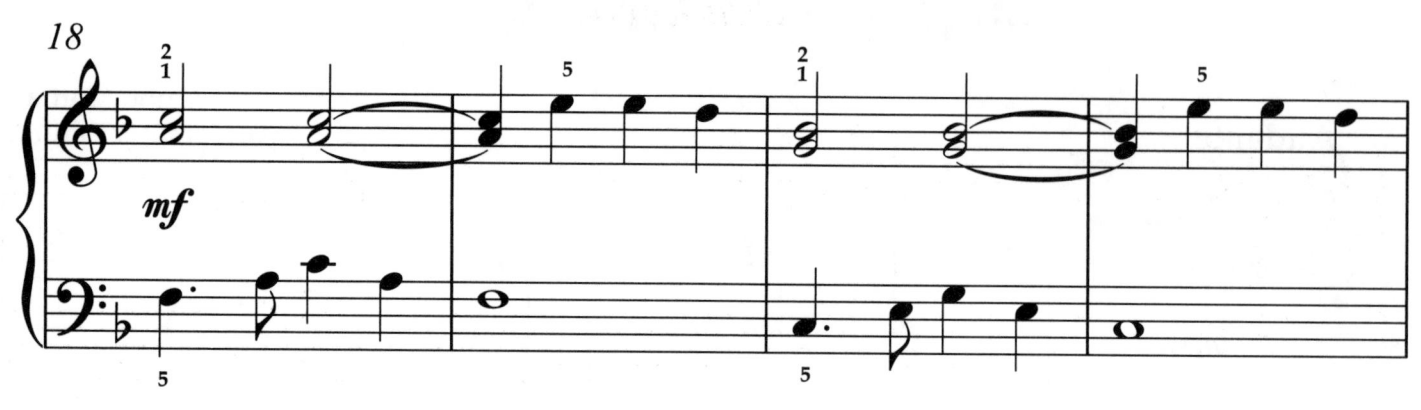
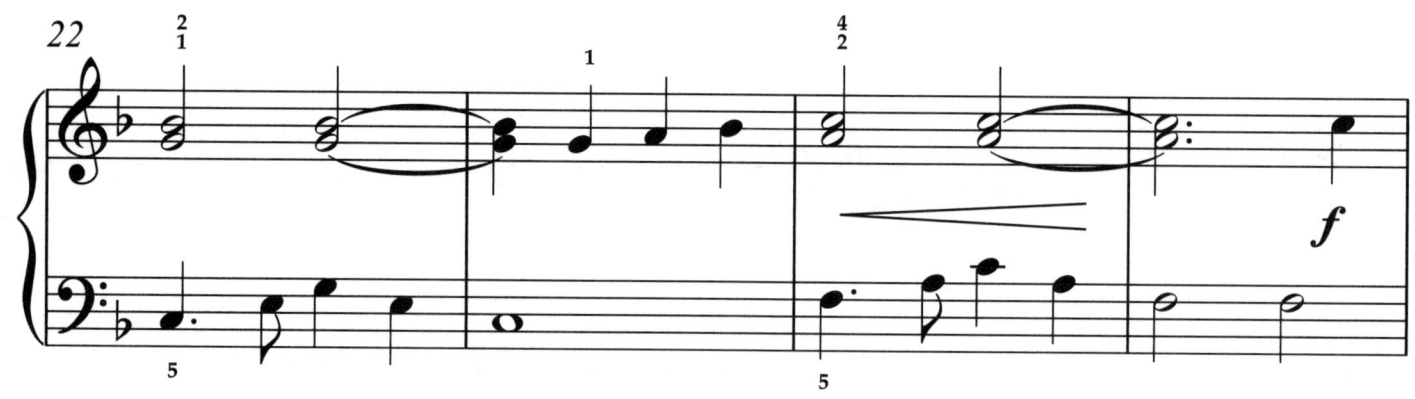
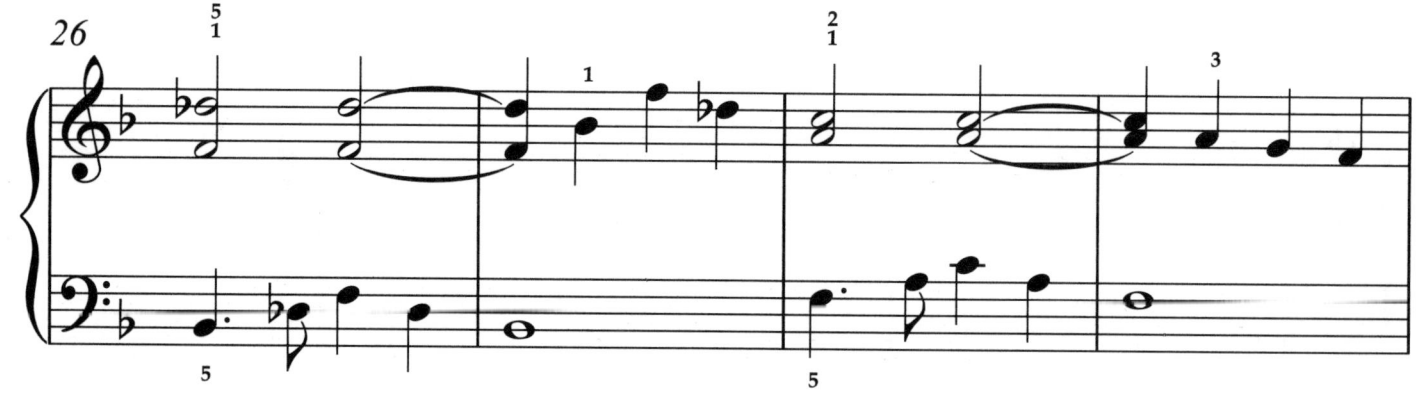
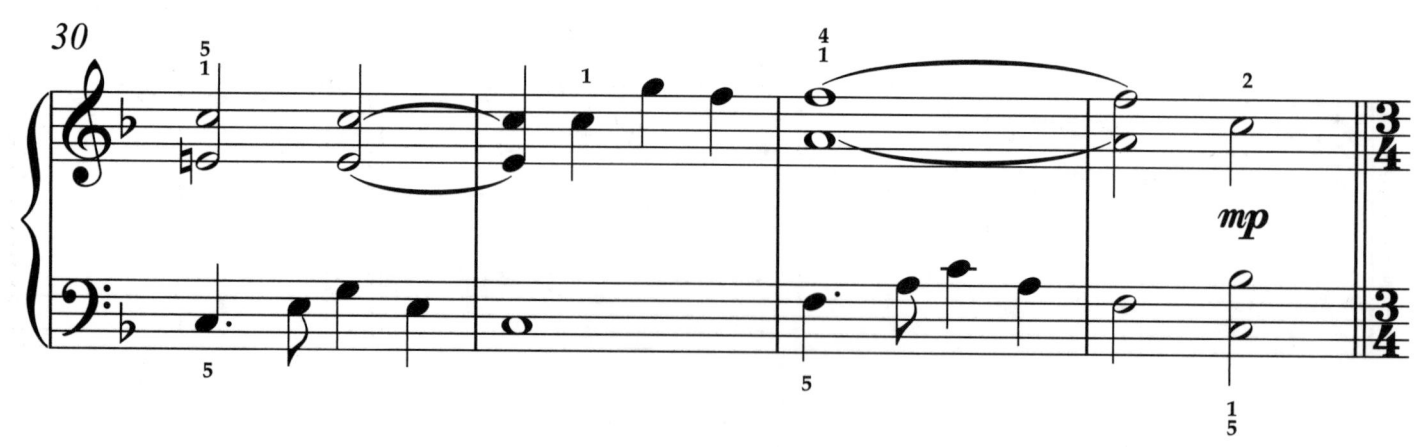

Santa Lucia

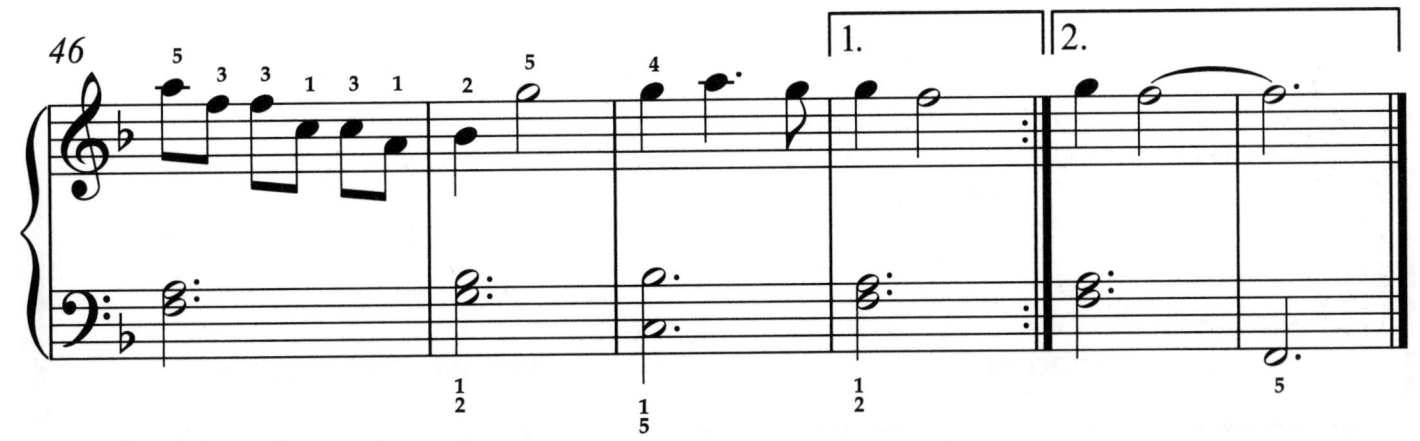

NEW TEMPO

Con spirito = Lively, with spirit.

NEW DYNAMIC MARKING

$f\!f$ = Fortissimo = Very loud

MATCHING

Allegretto	Fast
Presto	Gracefully
Grazioso	With spirit
Lento	Getting faster
Con spirito	Getting slower
Allegro	Light and cheerful
accelerando	Slow
a tempo	Very fast
ritardando	At the original tempo

PRONTO PREP

Play the examples below to help prepare for "*Caprice.*"

Caprice

Con Spirito

Niccolo Paganini
Arr. Jennifer Eklund

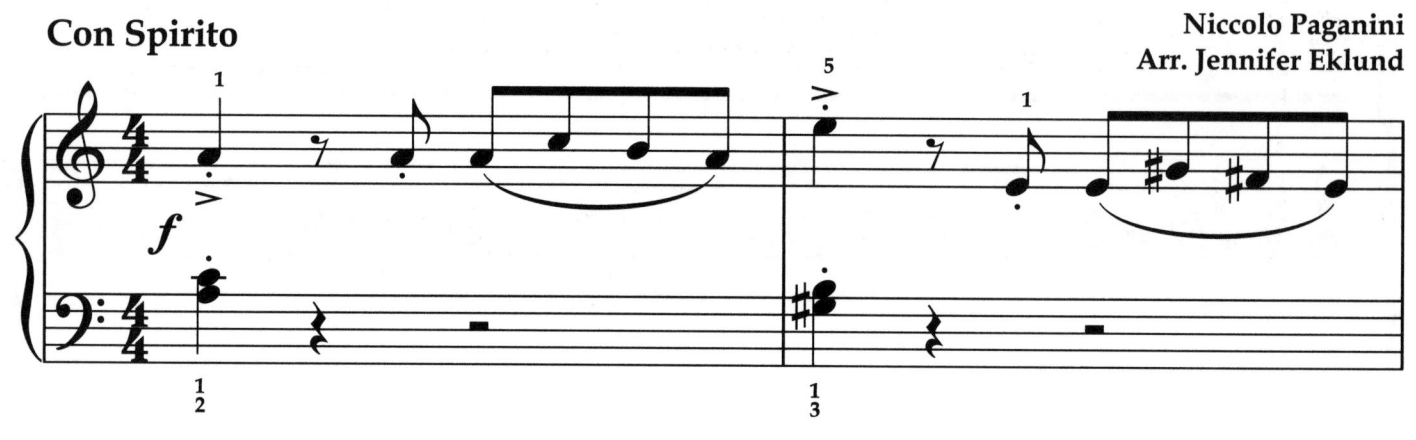
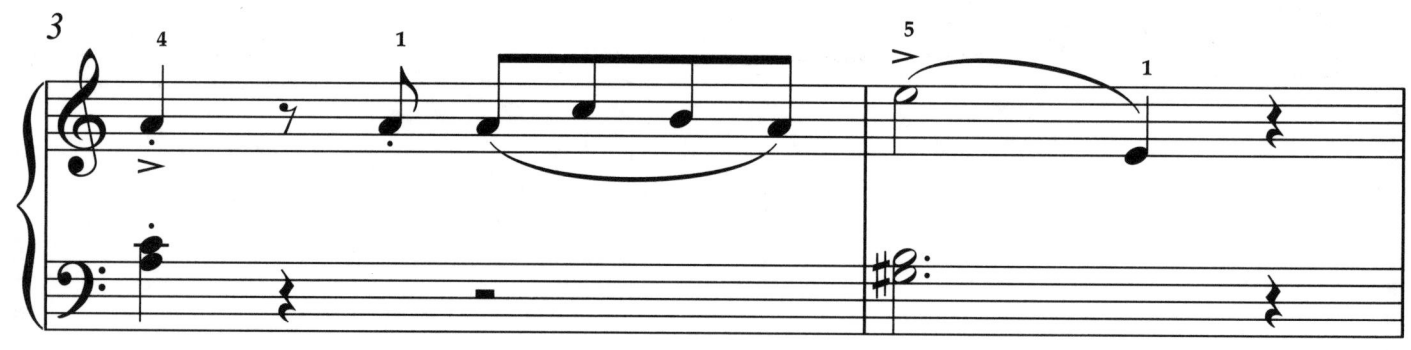

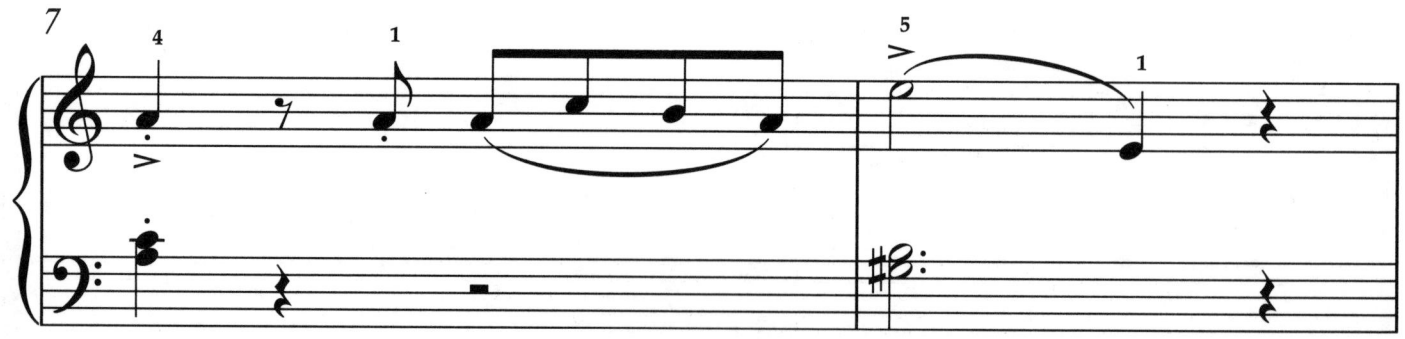

PRONTO PREP

Play the examples below to help prepare for "*Symphony #40 Theme.*"

BEFORE YOU BEGIN:

- The next piece is in the **key of:** _____

Symphony #40 Theme

Mozart
Arr. Jennifer Eklund

Allegro

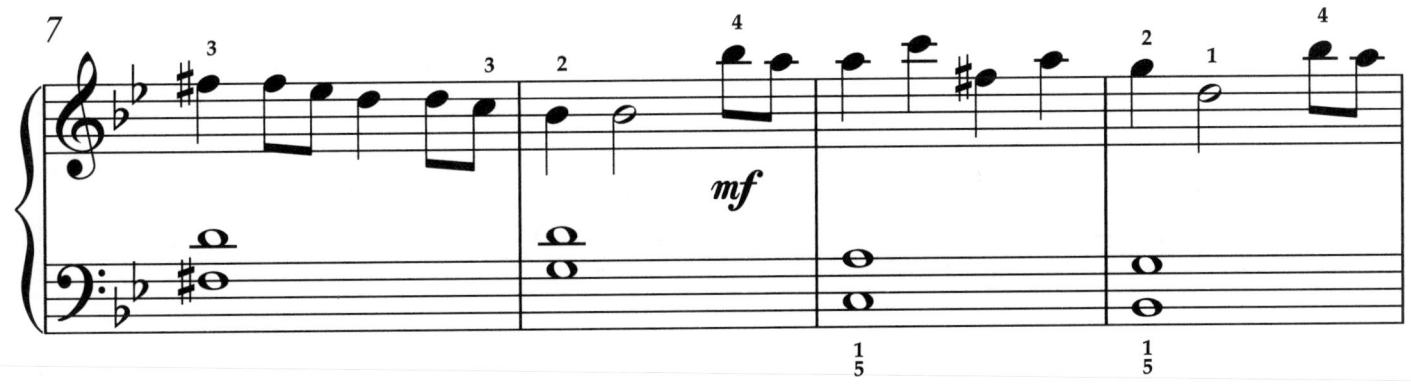

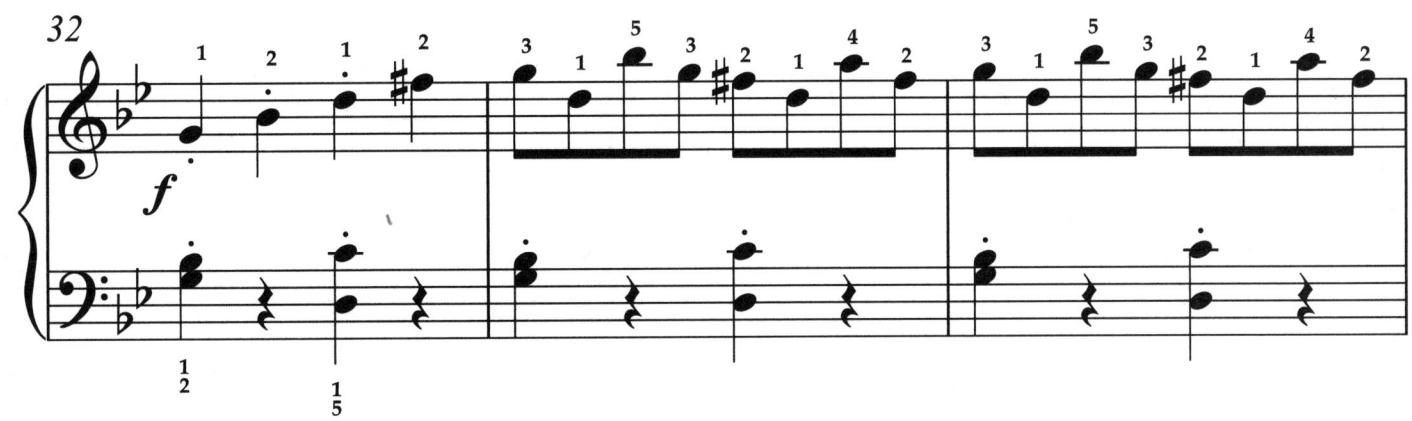
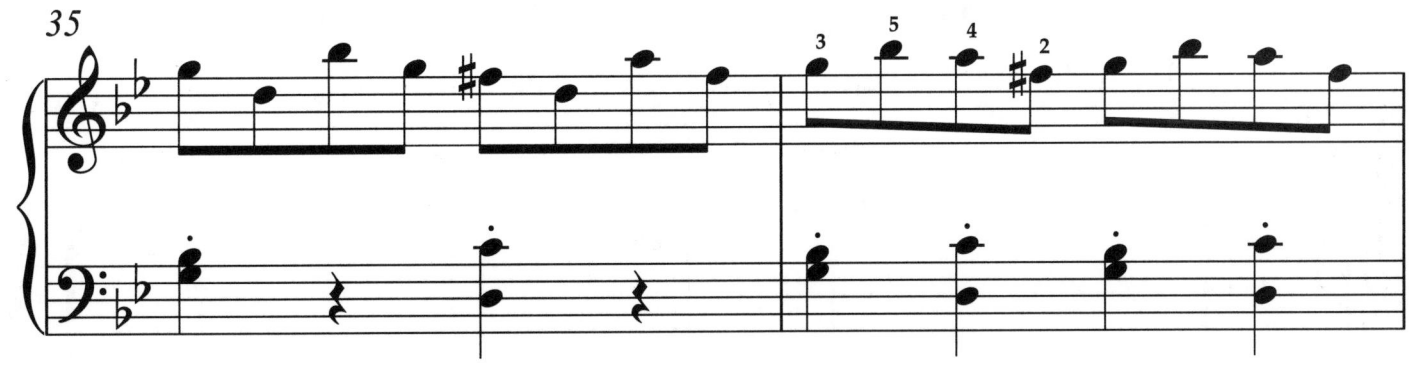
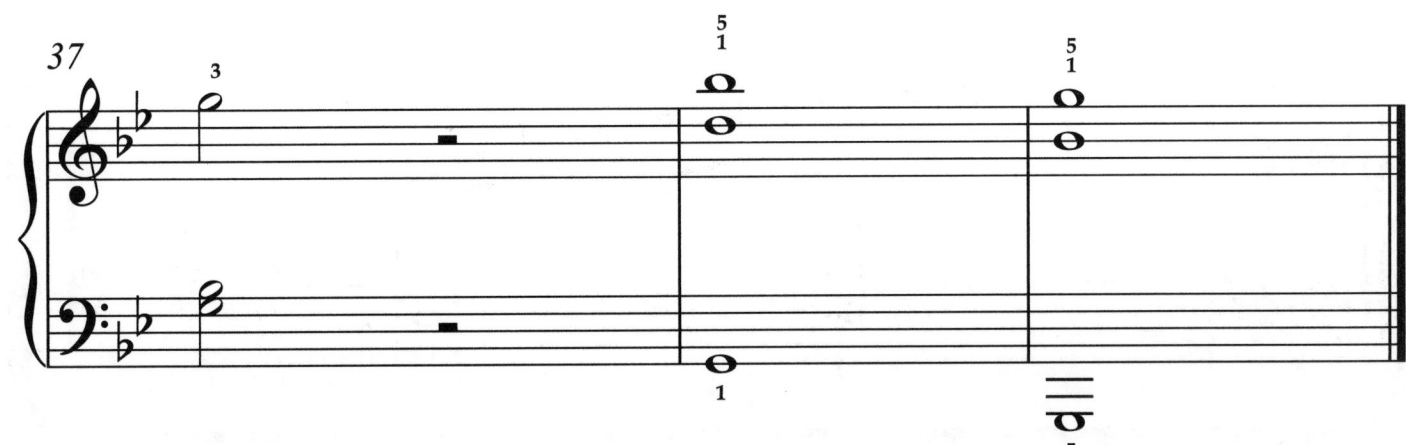

ARPEGGIO LINES

An arpeggio is a broken chord. Notes with an arpeggio line next to them are played on the beat and "rolled" from the bottom note to the top note. Look at the example below to see how an arpeggio line is notated.

Start at the low C and roll the chord upwards one note at a time. Hang on to the previous notes!

Now It's Your Turn

Play the examples below to practice chords with arpeggio lines.

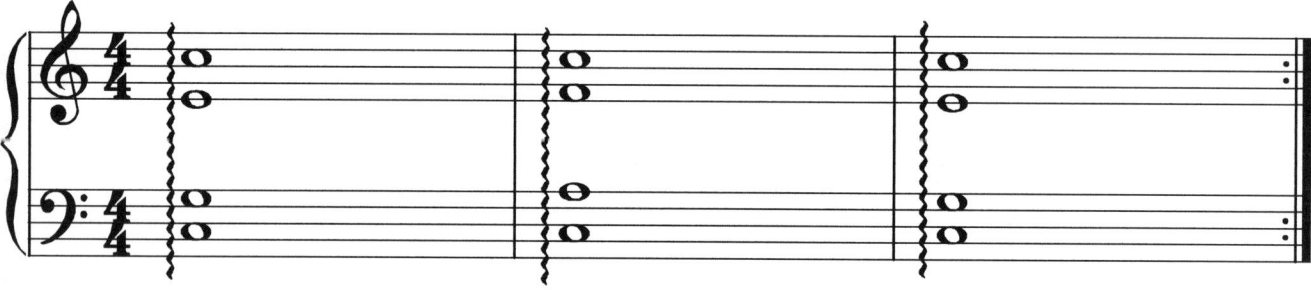

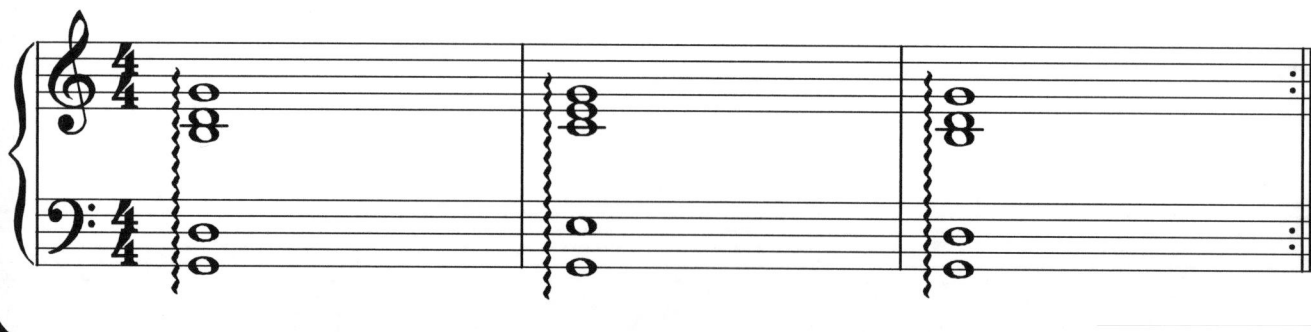

PRONTO PREP

Play the examples below to help prepare for "*Je te veux.*"

Je te veux
(I see you)

Erik Satie
Arr. Jennifer Eklund

Moderato

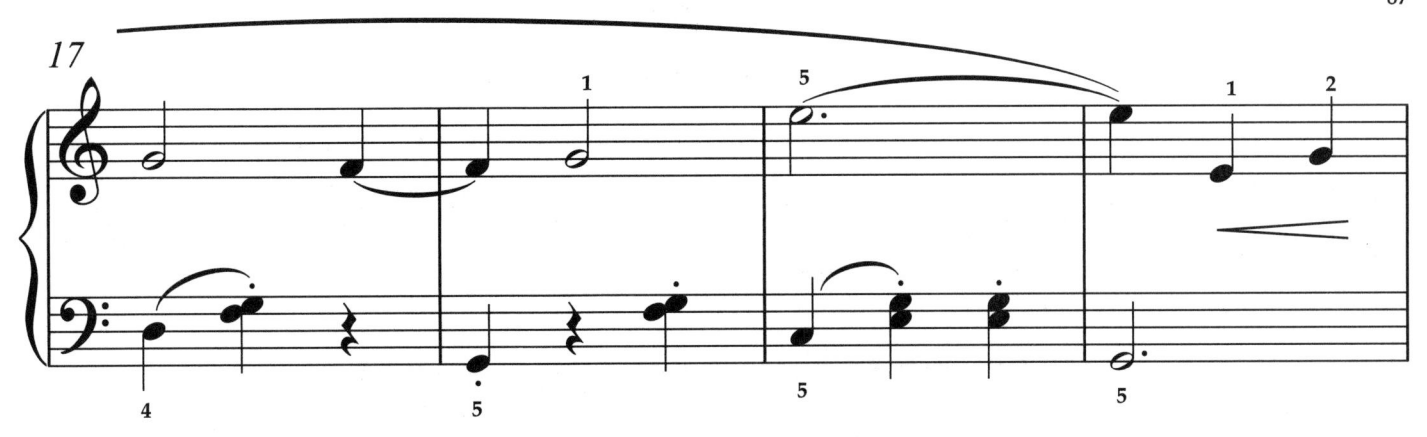

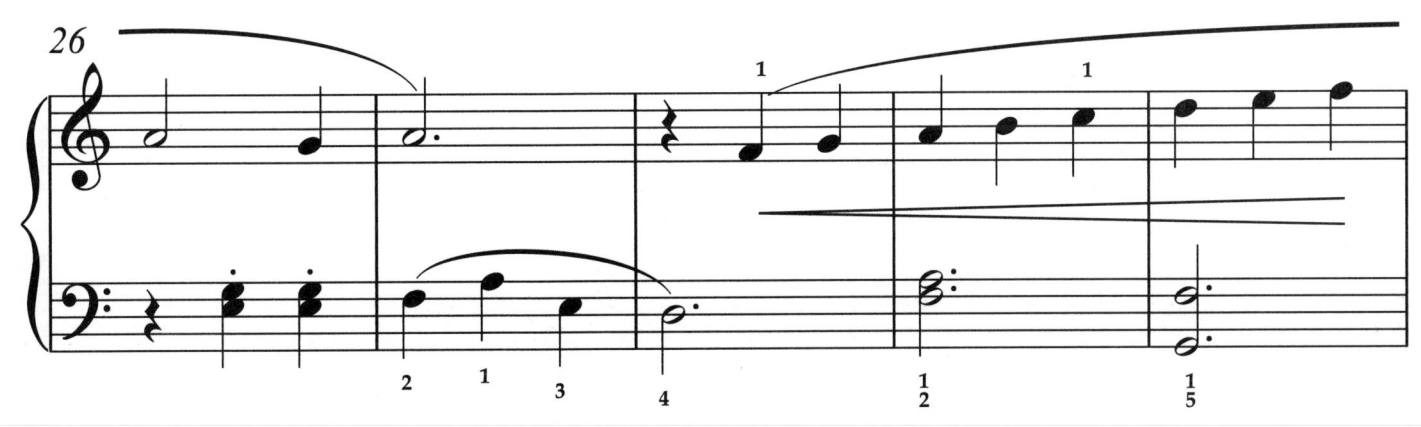
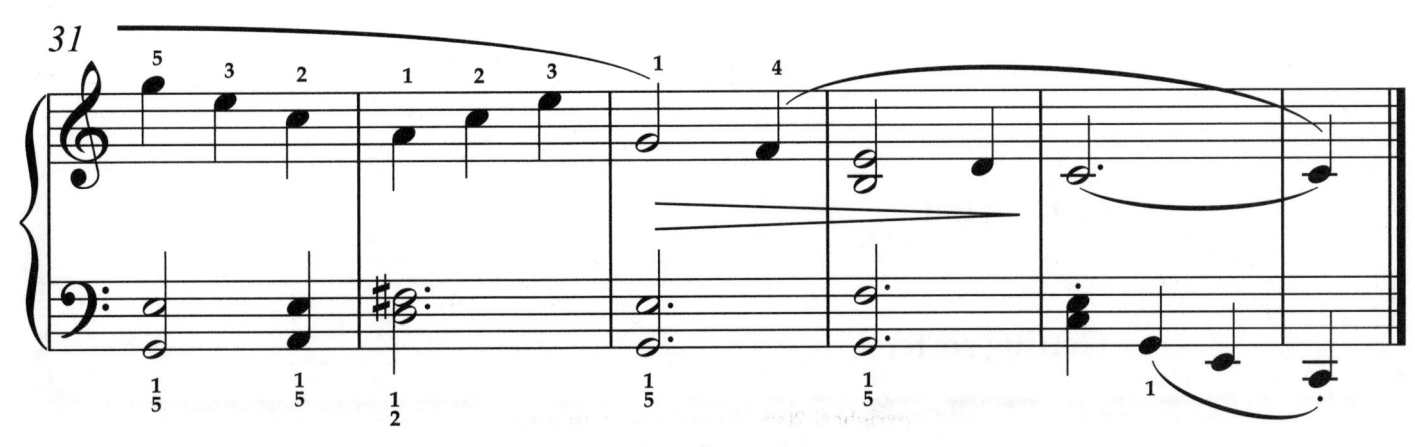

NEW TEMPO

Con moto = with motion

NEW DYNAMIC MARKING

pp = Pianissimo = Very soft

DYNAMICS CHART

Very Soft _____

Soft _____

Medium soft _____

Medium loud _____

Loud _____

Very Loud _____

Strong accent (*sforzando*) _____

Getting louder _____

Getting softer _____

PRONTO PREP

Play the examples below to help prepare for "*Fur Elise.*"

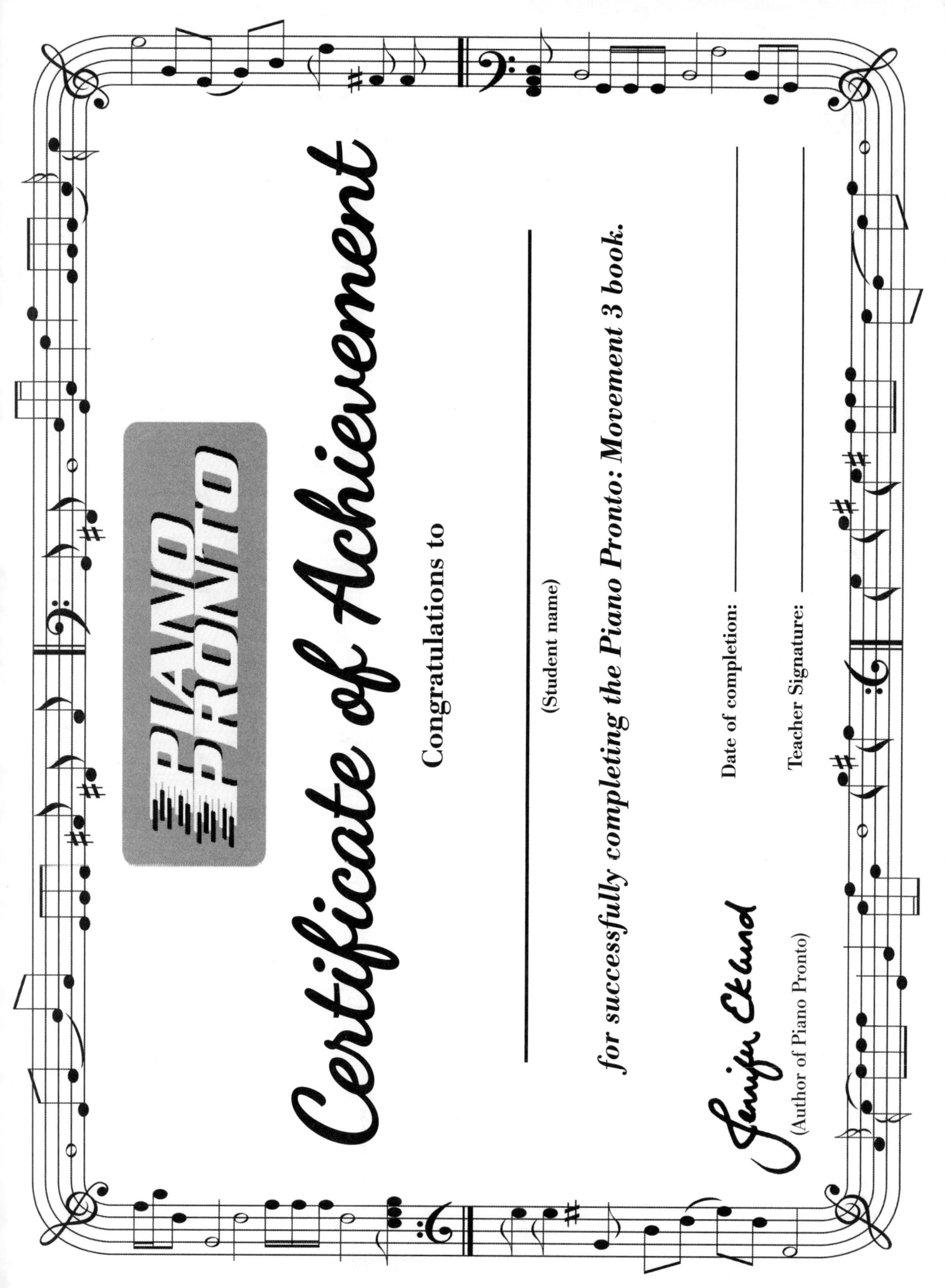